Using Content-Area Graphic Texts for Learning

A Guide for Middle-Level Educators

Meryl Jaffe and Katie Monnin

Using Content-Area Graphic Texts for Learning:
A Guide for Middle-Level Educators
By Meryl Jaffe & Katie Monnin

Cover Design: Studio Montage
Book Design and Layout: Rick Soldin

Library of Congress Cataloging-in-Publication Data

Jaffe, Meryl.
   Using content-area graphic texts for learning : a guide for middle-level educators / Meryl Jaffe & Katie Monnin.
          pages cm
   Includes bibliographical references and index.
   ISBN 978-1-936700-60-8 (pbk.)
   1. Reading (Middle school) 2. Content area reading. 3. Graphic novels--Study and teaching. I. Title.
   LB1632.J34 2013
   428.4071'2--dc23   2012037145

ISBN: 978–1–936700–60–8

Maupin House publishes professional resources for K-12 educators. Contact us for tailored, in-house training or to schedule an author for a workshop or conference. Visit www.maupinhouse.com for free lesson plan downloads.

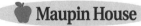 **Maupin House**

Maupin House Publishing, Inc.
2300 NW 71st Place
Gainesville, FL 32653
www.maupinhouse.com
800–524–0634
352–373–5588
352–373–5546 (fax)
info@maupinhouse.com

10 9 8 7 6 5 4 3 2 1

To the very best teachers—ever—Talia, Leah, Zev, and Adam. I love you and am so grateful to share this and so much more with you!

And to Rav Agbby, whose spiritual guidance continues to inspire us all.

Acknowledgments

From Meryl

This has been a spectacular journey for me, and I would like to thank my guides in chronological order. First, to my teachers, who encouraged and pushed me to meet my potential. Thank you, Susan Reimer Sacks, who convinced me to become a teacher, seeing strengths and skills in me that took many more years for me to recognize. Thank you, Dr. Glenn Snelbecker and Dr. Jeanette Gallagher, who continuously pushed my thinking, creating "disequilibriums" in my level of understanding, and facilitating avenues of pursuit to fill the newly wrenched "holes." A special thanks to Walter Schuchatowitz ("Mr. S."), principal of Bi-Cultural Day School, who gave me free reign on content and curriculum, and to my colleagues and students, who made teaching there so wonderful.

Thank you to my colleague Katie Monnin, whom I am so happy to call "friend" and with whom we thank our awesome editor, Emily Raij and publisher, Julie Graddy.

I want to thank my parents, Lloyd and Solange Jaffe, for their love and support. I am grateful you're here to share this and so much more with me. Thank you to my in-laws, Judy Kaufman Hurwich, who left this world way too early but whose critical literary voice still echoes in my head, and Baruch Hurwich, whose love and encouragement was also cut off way too soon. Last, but by no means least, I send my heartfelt love and gratitude to my children, Talia, Leah, and Zev, whose support, creative ideas, and blunt suggestions have helped me to be a better person, teacher, and parent. And to my husband, Adam, who provided support, encouragement, and direction—thank you for … everything!

From Katie

Meryl Jaffe is a phenomenal friend and co-author. This book was her idea, and I am so grateful she asked me to come along for this phenomenal writing journey. This book is truly written from the heart, inspired by the need to fill the gap in literacy scholarship about how content-area graphic novels can, indeed, be taught in the classroom.

I would also like to thank my parents, Ed and Judy Monnin. Now that I have gotten older, I finally realize how much both of you did (both in the past and in the present) to help me get where I wanted to be. Right here, right now: Teaching an appropriate three to four

professorial hours a day and then, like right now, sitting on the couch watching reality TV and writing books. Excellent job mom and dad! We should've seen it coming on my first day of kindergarten. An average preschooler does not come home from school worrying about "All My Children" and whether or not Palmer died today. Classic: "Mommy," through sobs, "did Palmer die today?"

My two inspirations, wiener dogs Sam and Max (or—when I drop them off with the dogsitter—also known as "Jesus" and "Hey-Seuss"). How else would the dogsitter know the importance of her dog-sitting job?

I would like to thank the following people for their contributions to both my career and my life: Dr. Nancy Padak; Dr. Wanda Hedrick; Dr. Stacy Boote; Josh, Sarah, and Cody Davis; Ken Hill; June Surette Cupp; Jordyn and Asher Monnin; Emily Raij; and, last but certainly not least, Julie Graddy.

Using Content-Area Graphic Texts for Learning

Contents

Introduction.. XI

Our Goals.. XII

How This Book Is Organized XII

Part I: Why Teach Young Adult Content-Area Graphic Novels? 1

Chapter 1: The Not-So-Secret Life of the Graphic Novel's Literary Power........... 3

But what does the education world have to say about graphic novels as
literary-level texts? 5

Putting the pieces together: The Golden Age of teaching young adult
content-area graphic novels 6

Chapter 2: Content-area Graphic Novel Terminology 101 11

Graphic novels 101.. 12

Figure 2.1: An example of a graphic novel panel from Vera Brosgol's *Anya's Ghost*
(First Second Books, 2011) 12

Figure 2.2: Eleven types of graphic novel panels, definitions, and examples 12

Figure 2.3: The six types of graphic novel gutters 16

Figure 2.4: The six types of graphic novel balloons..................... 18

Part II: Teaching Content-Area Graphic Texts.................................21

Figure 3.1: How graphic novels can help the five student profiles 24

Chapter 3: Graphic Novels in the Math Classroom 25

How graphic novels can help students in math: a general overview...................... 26

A math lesson using graphic novels as a math manipulative and motivational tool........ 26

Figure 3.2: Space to Earth ratio worksheet 29

The Laika lesson's demands 30

Figure 3.3: What is Ms. Fibonacci asking her students to do?..................... 31

Constructing a graphic novel page lesson plan 32

The lesson demands of constructing a graphic novel...................... 33

Figure 3.4: Instructions for designing a graphic novel page 35

Figure 3.5: What is involved in constructing graphic novels? 36

How graphic novels help our five students in math 37

Conclusion and suggested graphic novels for middle-school math instruction 40

Figure 3.6: A middle-level cross-index of thematically identified and
standards-aligned math graphic novels 40

Chapter 4: Graphic Novels in the Language Arts Classroom **43**

How graphic novels can help students in language arts: a general overview 43

Teaching reading with middle-level language arts graphic novels 44

Identifying the elements of story in both a traditional, print-text novel and
a contemporary graphic novel 45

Figure 4.1: "The Literate Eye" 46

Lesson demands informing teaching reading with *Smile* and *The Outsiders* 49

Figure 4.2: What is Mr. Merlin asking his students to do? 50

Figure 4.3: IRA/NCTE writing-based standards for teaching middle-level
language arts with graphic novels 52

Teaching writing with middle-level language arts graphic novels 52

A writing-focused graphic novel lesson plan for middle-level students and
their teachers 53

The lesson demands of writing an alternative graphic novel ending 60

Figure 4.4: Lesson demands emphasized in writing a graphic novel
alternative ending 61

How graphic novels help our five students in language arts 64

Conclusion and suggested graphic novels for middle-level language
arts instruction 66

Figure 4.5: Thematic list of middle-level language arts graphic novels 67

Chapter 5: Graphic Novels in the Social Studies Classroom **73**

How graphic novels help students in social studies: a general overview 74

A social studies lesson using graphic novels 75

Figure 5.1: World War II French occupation and propaganda worksheet 79

The lesson's demands 80

Figure 5.2: What is this lesson asking students to do? 82

How graphic novels help our five students in social studies 86

Conclusion and suggested graphic novels for middle-school
social studies instruction 87

Figure 5.3: A middle-level cross-index of thematically identified and
standards-aligned social studies graphic novels 88

Chapter 6: Graphic Novels in the Science Classroom 95

How graphic novels can help students in science: a general overview 96

Two ways to integrate graphic novels in the science classroom 97

Lesson option 1: Students critically read a science graphic novel 98

Figure 6.1: Science fact/science fiction/study further worksheet for
Squish #1: Super Amoeba 99

Figure 6.2: Demonstration of Squish: Amoeba Power worksheet 101

Lesson option 2: Students create their own science-fiction graphic novels 101

The lesson's demands 103

Figure 6.3: What is this lesson asking students to do? 105

How graphic novels help our five students in science 108

Conclusion and suggested graphic novels for middle-school science instruction 109

Figure 6.4: A middle-level cross-index of thematically identified and
standards-aligned science graphic novels 110

Appendix 113

References 135

Index 139

Introduction

"We're here for forty-five minutes. Have fun with the time, but don't even THINK about taking out any of those comics or graphic novels!"

—Meryl Jaffe

That is how I used to preface visits to the library or bookstore with my students and children.

In my mind, graphic novels were often violent collections about caped crime-fighters, masked madmen, or fictional friends at Riverdale High School. How did I know this? That's what the comic books of my childhood were all about, and I hadn't seen anything different to change my mind. Admittedly, I hadn't been looking to change my mind. *Johnny Tremain, Of Mice and Men,* and *The Gammage Cup* were just fine for my middle schoolers. These books created worlds of fantasy or historical fiction that made my readers think, while incorporating language in inspiring ways. I realize now, though, that reading lists, like most things in life, can't remain static. They must be fluid, dynamically bending and adjusting to the time and winds of change.

A few years ago, my children sat me down and passionately argued that in any discussion of literacy, graphic novels had to be included. I reluctantly agreed to read one book of their choice. With the stakes high, I advised them to choose wisely, and they did. They selected Joe Kelly's *I Kill Giants,* and I was truly blown away. As Kelly's story opens, the reader meets Barbara, a fifth-grade girl who explains that she kills giants. The thing is, it takes most of the book to determine whether this is a metaphor for something bigger, stronger, and scarier in her life or she actually kills giants. He leaves it to you (and your students) to figure out which is the case.

Katie and I come to you from different perspectives. She began her career in the classroom and is now in academia; I began in academia and am now in the classroom. She is a young, vibrant rising star, and I am a seasoned parent, a school psychologist, and an educator. Although we both came to graphic novels relatively recently in our professional careers, we have become strong advocates for their inclusion in today's classrooms and libraries.

While Katie and I discuss the movement of graphic novels from comic book shops to the classroom in Part I of this book, there have been three general factors that led us, personally, to include them in our classrooms:

1. There is now a wealth of motivating, high-quality graphic novels (be they fiction, science fiction, historical fiction, fantasy, or nonfiction) that lend themselves to content-area classroom use.

2. With the growth of technology and access to the Internet, there is now an increasing need for visual and verbal literacy mastery, emphasized not only in our everyday lives, but also in the Common Core State Standards.

3. Graphic novels, by their very nature, draw the reader into the story, because the reader must construct the story by actively integrating visual and verbal components. This is a highly creative and interactive process, which makes learning more meaningful.

Our Goals

While teaching methods and goals are rapidly expanding to meet the demands of our ever shrinking—and yet expanding—worlds, we hope to empower you with specific tools to meet those demands. Educators are now mandated to address visual and verbal literacies by incorporating multimodal texts and sources, while fostering greater independent, creative, and analytic thinking. To help address these needs and changes, we offer you concrete teaching options in the form of interactive graphic novel suggestions and lesson plans. Graphic novels provide an excellent vehicle to meet curricular standards while incorporating diverse student needs and affinities.

Our goal in this book is to introduce you to today's graphic novels. We explain how they have matured, how they address learning and curriculum standards, and, finally, how they can be taught in your content-area middle-school classrooms. We also demonstrate how graphic novels and our suggested lessons meet diverse student needs featuring attention, memory, language, sequencing, and cognition skills.

How This Book Is Organized

In the first part of this book, we introduce you to the mechanics of today's graphic novels and detail how they have changed throughout the years. We also relate why these books are such effective teaching tools for modern classrooms.

The second part of this book takes you to our four content-area classrooms: math, language arts, social studies, and science. Each content-area chapter:

✦ Explains how graphic novels can meet your curricular needs;

✦ Provides two types of lessons, each using graphic novels in a different way;

◆ Demonstrates what each lesson asks students to do—focusing on attention, memory, language, sequencing, and cognition skills;

◆ Shows each lesson's alignment with the Common Core State Standards;

◆ Discusses how graphic novels in our lessons help different types of students succeed in the content-area classroom; and

◆ Includes a list of other suggested graphic novels you can include in your content-area classroom.

Please note, however, that the lessons and suggested readings we provide are merely suggestions. We encourage you to expand upon these suggested readings and tweak our lessons to meet your own personal teaching preferences and student needs. And, if you are so inclined, we hope you share your explorations and experiences with these lessons and suggested readings with us at www.departingthetext.blogspot.com. Check the blog for new lessons, graphic novel reviews, content-area classroom tips, conference appearances, and more.

Why Teach Young Adult Content-Area Graphic Novels?

Part I of *Using Content-Area Graphic Texts for Learning* identifies and reviews the theoretical and historical insights as to why twenty-first-century, middle-level educators should teach content-area graphic novels. The major topics in Part I of *Using Content-Area Graphic Texts for Learning* are designed to help teachers better understand why this book is so necessary to today's educators and their students. In particular, Part I introduces the history and power of graphic novels in education and models how to advocate and integrate graphic novels into the middle-school curriculum.

In Chapter 1, you'll discover the not-so-secret life of the graphic novel's content-area reading powers, see what the education world has to say about graphic novels as literary-level texts, and put the pieces together to take part in the "Golden Age" of teaching young adult, content-area graphic novels. Chapter 2 lists and defines graphic novel terminology 101, your building blocks for teaching content-area graphic novels.

The Not-So-Secret Life of the Graphic Novel's Literary Power

A very interesting phenomenon in today's young adult literary world revolves around the graphic novel. As one of the most popular young adult literary formats, the graphic novel is coming of age right alongside its largest reading audience. According to contemporary reading research, young adults are reading graphic novels in record numbers. And, as if that is not enough, young-adult graphic novels are being published in record numbers on a variety of topics and in a variety of genres and content areas. From the fiction and nonfiction graphic novels to scientific, historical, and mathematical graphic novels for young adults, they are available for all types of readers and their teachers.

Before we discuss the vast array of graphic novels now available for young adults and their teachers and how to effectively integrate them into your classrooms, we would like to back up and first answer two questions teachers often ask:

1. "Are graphic novels really a valid young-adult literary format?"

2. "Do graphic novels belong in content-area classrooms?"

Purposefully named and formatted to differentiate itself from the traditional comic book, the term "graphic novel" evolved after the 1954 publication of Frederic Wertham's *Seduction of the Innocent*. Claiming that comics were a cause of juvenile delinquency, Wertham's *Seduction of the Innocent* tainted and poisoned the perceptions many Americans had not only regarding comic books themselves, but also the entire comic book industry (writers and artists included). And the comic book industry responded.

Feeling as though they were spending their time genuinely caring about and writing for their young readers, many writers and artists felt Wertham's research was not just inaccurate, but also faulty. First, Wertham grouped all comic books into one category: crime comics. Of course, this was not true. There were, and still are, many subgenres of comics; in fact, a few of these subgroups will later be shown in this book to contain age-appropriate, high-quality, and literary-level content-area graphic novels. Second, Wertham's work did not qualify as scientific research. There was no scientific study or method. Wertham simply interviewed criminals and asked them what they read. When they cited comic books, he noted them. By no reach of the imagination—either today or when it was published—does such questioning and answering qualify as empirical scientific research.

In fact, during the decade leading up to Wertham's publication of *Seduction of the Innocent*— the 1940s—eighty to 100 million comic books were sold per week. On top of that, each comic book sold was likely passed along to another six to ten readers. If we multiply eighty million readers by six more readers, the lower of the two numbers, we get 480 million readers. In the 1940s and 1950s, it was pretty difficult to find any child who wasn't reading comic books. That said, Wertham's claim that comic books influenced juvenile delinquency then becomes faulty on a third ground. Pretty much every juvenile in America in the 1940s and 1950s was reading comic books, and the vast majority of them grew up to be healthy, happy, and law-abiding adults (Hadju, 2008).

Luckily, for the comic book industry, some of its key members organized and sought to respond to the faulty, seed-bearing notions of Wertham's *Seduction of the Innocent*. Seeking to prove that images and words could work together to tell a literary-level story, many comic book writers and artists began to throw around some proactive ideas that would eventually lead to the term "graphic novel." And although it's difficult to determine who exactly coined the term "graphic novel," most graphic novel scholars credit Will Eisner and his 1978 publication of the first graphic novel, *The Contract with God*.

The purpose behind the graphic novel, as Eisner and many other comic artists point out, is to show that sequential images and the written word can work together on a literary level. Eisner's *Comics and Sequential Art* (1985) states that the graphic novel's use of images and words actually call on the reader to think on two literary levels: "The regimens of art … and the regimens of literature … [as they] become superimposed upon each other. The reading of the comic book [or graphic novel] is an act of both aesthetic perception and intellectual pursuit" (p. 8). Eleven years later, in 1996, Eisner's *Graphic Storytelling and Visual Narrative* further noted that graphic novels involved a more intense reading experience than traditional print-text literature:

> In text alone the process of reading involves word-to-image conversion. Comics [and graphic novels] accelerates that by providing the image. When properly executed, it goes beyond conversion and speed and becomes a seamless whole. In every sense, this misnamed [misunderstood] form of reading is entitled to be regarded as literature. (p. 5)

Contemporary graphic novelist and scholar Scott McCloud, Eisner's mentee in the graphic novel world, also explained how and why graphic novels are, indeed, literary-level texts. McCloud's 2007 *Making Comics* states that graphic novels—perhaps even more so than the single literacy-based text—are literary on two levels: "Words and pictures can combine to create effects that neither could create separately" (p. 4). Together, Eisner and McCloud are two of the most direct and outspoken advocates for graphic novels as literary texts.

But what does the education world have to say about graphic novels as literary-level texts?

Since the 1990s, contemporary literacy scholarship has built upon this idea of teaching multiple literacies, and one of the literacies to receive significant attention has, indeed, been the visual mode. Modern literacy education needs to better reflect a shared literacy stage (Kress, 2003; Monnin, 2010, 2011). Picture an empty stage and yourself as the director of the upcoming play. As director, you need to fill two starring roles. Contemporary literacy educators argue that the two leading actors in your play need to be print-text literacy and image literacy.

Because we are living during the greatest communication revolution of all time (second historically, but not significantly, to the fifteenth-century invention of the printing press), today's students no longer primarily encounter only print-text literacies. They encounter a more balanced literacy stage —a stage on which being able to read and write with print-text is just as important as being able to read and write with both print-text and image-text literacies together (Kress, 2003; Monnin, 2010, 2011). Due to advancements in technologies that place equal value on reading and writing from print-text and image-text literacies (mp3 players, tablets, film, animation, television, cell phones, the Internet, text and video messaging, and hypermedia, just to name a few), modern students must be competent with both types of literacies. Their teachers must also become competent with these two major co-starring literacies.

Perhaps the most well-respected, contemporary scholar on teaching print-text literacies alongside image literacies, Kress (2003) explains: "The world told is a different world to the world shown" (p. 1). Carter's (2007) *Building Literacy Connections with Graphic Novels* responds to Kress' idea that educators teach both the told and the shown worlds, by calling for a re-evaluation of what counts as literacy in twenty-first-century classrooms:

> To understand thoroughly the promise of the graphic novel as an aide to more conventional notions of literacy, it is important to review what the notion of literacy signifies in contemporary talk and practice …. Obviously, the graphic novel can offer a rich and stimulating means by which to develop the visual literacy of students. As more research on dual coding develops, sequential art seems destined to have an even more prominent place in the English language arts classroom. (p. 7–13)

David Booth's (2006) *Reading Doesn't Matter Anymore* also claims that graphic novels—which use sequential art to tell a story—deserve a more prominent place in the language arts classroom. Booth, however, argues that along with knowing that new literacies such as graphic novels should be taught in contemporary classrooms, teachers should also be aware of their new status as literacy change agents:

> We need to see literacy as a series of processes that can offer us a means, a pathway, to deeper, more complex understandings and constructions of our

own worlds. The value of literacy education, both inside and outside schools, involves what we do with what we learn, and with whom we live … Our traditional way of thinking about and defining literacy will be insufficient if we hope to provide youngsters with what they will need to be full participants in the world of the future. (p. 11–12)

Amidst the greatest communication revolution of all time, today's teachers are being asked to be literacy change agents. For the first time in the history of education, teachers will need to redefine what counts as literacy in modern classrooms.

"But wait," we are often asked at this point, "are you saying that today's teachers need to leave print-text literacies behind and teach only new, primarily image-based literacies?"

Our answer is always *absolutely not*. It goes back to the shared literacy stage. Like Carter and Booth, we are simply trying to point out that image-based literacies (or any other new literacy for that matter) now share the stage with traditional, print-text literacies. In the case of the graphic novel, that means that while content-area teachers will most likely continue to use their traditional textbooks, they now have the opportunity to complement and enhance those textbooks by pairing them with a related content-area graphic novel.

To date, almost all of the classroom practice and research with graphic novels has occurred in language arts classrooms. In 2007, five years before the writing of this book, Carter inspired teachers from all content areas to think more broadly about the literary scope and potential of graphic novels: "There is a graphic novel for virtually every learner … just as comics experienced a 'a Golden Age' of popularity in the 1940s, comics and the graphic novel are experiencing a burgeoning Golden Age in education today" (Carter, p. 1). Since 2007, graphic novels have indeed continued to experience a burgeoning Golden Age in education, and Carter was right. There is a graphic novel for every learner in every content area.

Inspired by Carter and the growing number of content-area graphic novels being published each day, we are extremely excited to share *Using Content-Area Graphic Texts for Learning* with you. Focused specifically on young-adult graphic novels in the four primary content areas—science, social studies, math, and language arts—*Using Content-Area Graphic Texts for Learning* aims to empower twenty-first-century, middle-school educators to not only better understand content-area graphic novels, but also to teach content-area graphic novels.

Putting the pieces together: The Golden Age of teaching young adult content-area graphic novels

We would just like to take a few more moments in this chapter to put all the pieces together. So far, we know that a graphic novel is different from and more literary than a comic book. We also know that most language arts educators have already begun to teach content-area

graphic novels within their own scope and curriculum. But why is it so important to include graphic novels in all of the content areas? And why now? Is there an historical precedent or reason? In other words, how can content-area teachers explain why they should now teach content-area graphic novels in their classrooms?

Somewhat surprisingly, the answers are right in front of us. Across cultures, languages, and time, from our ancestors' times to today, being literate has first and foremost relied on image-based forms of communication (e.g., hieroglyphics, stone tablet writings, cave drawings, wall murals, etc.). When you think about it, even the alphabet is based on graphic symbols. Each letter represents a sound. And when we put these representative sounds together, they make up words—a string of image-represented sounds, if you will.

Given this historical precedent for reading and writing with both words and images, however, there still seems to be a gap between the past and the present. Somewhere between now and ancient times when hieroglyphics and other image-based communication systems shared the literacy stage, a movement occurred to label print-text—alphabetic letters—a seemingly more worthwhile and "established" form of communication.

There are multiple factors that led to the reliance of print to relay information. In part, there were too many diverse ideas and concepts that did not have universal pictures to represent them. As a result, these types of words were broken down into phonemes (basic sounds). This, in turn, led to the idea of communicating with print. The advent of the printing press sealed the deal. With the fifteenth-century invention of the printing press, "books" went from being rare, hand-written scrolls and individually-bound volumes (available only to the rich or the monks who wrote them) to mass-produced, recognizable, easy-to-find, household items and educational tools.

In the history of teaching English language arts in the United States, this focus on print-text literacies took on an even more significant role in the 1890s when a group of educators, who called themselves The Committee of Ten, were charged with deciding what types of literature students should read. Whether they intended to finish grade school or go on to college, the Committee of Ten, led by a collection of highly educated academic elites whose most noteworthy member and chair was Charles Eliot (president of Harvard University at the time), had some very specific recommendations. Students should read, as Eliot described, all the books that he had on a five-foot bookshelf in his office. This bookshelf full of print-text literacy books written by mostly white, British men helped Eliot's Committee of Ten set up a canonical view of what should be read in U.S. classrooms (Hart & Benson, 1996; Leavis & Thompson, 1933): print-text books written by white men of elite standing. Period.

While it may feel as though Eliot's influence on the U.S. view of what counts as literature has retained some of its power, many significant organizations and cross-content-area scholars have historically disagreed. The National Council of Teachers of English, founded in 1911, claimed that teachers should teach more than just these canonical texts; in fact, teachers should consider both their own and their students' interests when choosing literary texts.

In the 1920s and 1930s, literary scholars I.A. Richards and Louise Rosenblatt further pushed the boundaries of what types of literary texts should be brought into classrooms. Under the theoretical lens of Reader Response Theory, Richards (1929) and Rosenblatt (1938) dispelled the idea that even if teachers and/or students chose a literary text to their liking, they did not have to read that text with an eye toward authorial intent. According to Richards' and Rosenblatt's Reader Response Theory, readers could come to a literary text with their own, unique personal experiences and history in mind and, because of those unique identities, interpret literary texts through their own personal lenses. As a result, the role of books in the classroom began to change.

In the second half of the twentieth century, literary scholars expanded Reader Response Theory in two complementary directions. First, literary scholars encouraged teachers to introduce diverse cultural and social texts into their classrooms, thus opening up a whole new set of reading experiences and critical lenses for students and teachers to discuss (Appleman, 2000). Second, and beginning in the early 1930s (Langer, 1996; Leavis & Thompson, 1933; Maloney, 1960), literary scholars began to place emphasis on reading print-text literacies alongside image literacies.

In 1933, Leavis and Thompson stated that the popular emergence of film and film literacies should be taught in classrooms. But Leavis and Thompson were a bit ahead of their time. It was not until the 1960s to the 1980s—especially in response to the continued popularity of film and the ever-emerging ownership of televisions at home—that literacy scholars really began to take note and integrate image literacies into the classroom (Clark, 1983; Fehlman, 1992; Hobbs, 2007; Kist, 2004, 2009; Kress, 2003; The New London Group, 1996; *The Newsom Report*, 1963).

In 1963, British researchers published *The Newsom Report*. Charged with investigating the literacy abilities of both average and slightly below-average young adults, *The Newsom Report* found that half of the students reported feeling marginalized by the standard, print-text literacy school curriculum. Specifically, students felt as though the standard print-text literacy curriculum did not reflect their real literacy lives outside of school. Grounded in student suggestions and in their own scholarship on new literacies of film and television, *The Newsom Report* concluded by suggesting that all content-area teachers consider reaching out to more image-based, visual literacies. But, yet again, a bit ahead of its time, *The Newsom Report* made a small splash in what was to become a very large pond.

Five years later, and again addressed to all content-area educators, Freire's (1968) *Pedagogy of the Oppressed* also argued that teachers embrace diverse literacies. But in Freire's case, the reason for doing so was not only because of the growing popularity of image and visual-based literacies in film and television, but also because doing so would promote democratic classrooms where students' literacies of choice were integrated and complemented by the mandated curriculum.

In the 1970s, literacy education surged with research to support the need to bring image literacies into content-area classrooms. Howell's (1973) *Art Versus Entertainment in the Mass Media* and Amelio's (1976) *American Genre Film: Teaching Popular Movies* both posited that when cross-content-area educators brought visual and/or image literacies into the classroom, student engagement increased. Altschuler (1968) noted, however, that

> The users of popular media (that is, art films, comedy tapes, full-length feature entertainments) need not abandon the written word. What is needed is a reassessment of those things we have always believed could be done best by English teachers and a selection from among them of what we want to do with film. (p. 340)

Image and visual literacy education, Altschuler pointed out, should complement and share the stage with print-text literacies.

And the research of the 1980s and 1990s concurred. Masterman's (1985) *Teaching the Media* is considered the most seminal and significant text to further support the adoption of image literacies across content-area teaching: "We shall need to be not simply teachers of, but *advocates for* our subject, *advancing* its cause whenever we can within our own institutions, amongst parents and with colleagues and policy makers" (p. 20; emphasis in original). Teachers need to be, in other words, advocates for social literacy reform. Within their classrooms and within their communities, teachers need to explain why they are now teaching a shared literacy stage.

Pool (1983) also shared Masterman's concern:

> The onus is on us to determine whether free societies in the twenty-first century will conduct electronic communication under the conditions of freedom established for the domain of print through centuries of struggle, or whether that great achievement will become lost in a confusion about new technologies. (p. 10)

Like Freire and Masterman, Pool felt that teaching a shared literacy stage that values both print-text and image literacies was a matter of democratic freedom. If we truly live in a democracy, Pool points out, we will adapt our teaching to respect, value, and teach the democratic literacies of our own time in history; we will not simply teach one type of literacy because it has been dominant since the fifteenth century. Five hundred years ago—in the fifteenth-century—history called on us to adapt to and embrace print-text literacies. Now, history calls on us to adapt to and teach a shared literacy stage that values print-text literacies alongside image literacies.

The most significant splash in the waters of multi-literacy education, however, came in 1996.

In that year, The New London Group argued that educators embrace a pedagogy of multi-literacies to prepare contemporary students for the reality of the literacy world in which they now live (and will eventually work). To really grasp the significance of such a statement, let us offer you two quick anecdotes: While The New London Group was drafting its article, and only one year before it published its multi-literacy predictions, we were being introduced to a couple of novel means of communication: email and the World Wide Web! Katie, then entering college, was sent a letter that stated when students arrived in the fall, they would be the first class to "have an email account." That same summer day, her soon-to-be new college roommate called her, and they laughed their heads off about how ridiculous this "email" thing was. "Who," they laughed uproariously, "would ever go to one of these 'computer stations' to get an 'email?'" Meryl, working as a middle-school teacher, was sent to a teacher workshop to learn how to "surf" for classroom resources and teach with a revolutionary program called "Microsoft PowerPoint!"

Today, a mere fifteen years have passed, and our entire way of communicating and teaching has changed globally. The ways we read and write do consist of what The New London Group labeled "a pedagogy of multi-literacies." We read from screen- and image-dominant environments every day. Contemporary television, film, computers, the Internet, laptops, cell phones, iPods, iPads, graphic novels, magazines, billboards, and so on equally rely on both print-text and image literacies to convey information. And the corresponding and most significant research on literacy since 1996 and The New London Group's advocacy concurs.

Perhaps the most prominent and powerful voice on new literacy studies, Kress (2003), as noted previously in this chapter, states that modern educators must teach both a *told* and a *shown* world. Today's teacher must teach both print-text and image literacies, a pedagogy of multi-literacies. Buckingham (2003) and Hobbs' (2007) work on media education, and its emphases on the told and shown worlds, agrees. Today's teacher must adapt to the changed, revolutionized literacy world. As Kress puts it, contemporary education must mirror and better reflect the world outside of school. Educators must now teach to the greatest communication revolution of all time. It's a new day—a day we have never before experienced as educators—and that's exactly where a book like *Using Content-Area Graphic Texts for Learning* comes into play.

The bottom line: today's teacher must teach a shared literacy stage, a stage that students encounter both in and out of school. This contemporary literacy stage will better balance the literacy lives our students will lead after they depart from our classrooms and go on to live, work, and operate with both print text and visual text on a day-to-day basis—perhaps even more so than they do today. We hope, through this resource, to help teachers better address what it means to read and live in a multi-literate world.

Chapter 2

Content-area Graphic Novel Terminology 101

Because contemporary graphic novels reach out to diverse learners and their particular reading strengths, they are perfect, high-quality, literary-level texts that can be used in core content-area classrooms.

Complementary to their ability to reach out to diverse literacy learners, graphic novels also reinforce traditional content-area thinking skills, such as memory, attention, cognition, language learning, and sequencing. In fact, to emphasize the graphic novel's dual ability to reinforce and address multiple intelligences and traditional content-area learning skills, we will later introduce five students, each of whom exhibits weaknesses in one of these learning skills. We will pair each of these skills with a specific student profile, all of which you will likely recognize among your own students:

- ✦ Memory Megan
- ✦ Attention Andy
- ✦ Cognitive Coby
- ✦ Language Larry
- ✦ Sequencing Sue

By focusing on these students' reading and learning strengths, we will identify how content-area teachers can successfully incorporate graphic novels to address learning needs and preferences, making reading and learning more meaningful and effective.

But first, we need a little "graphic novels 101" to equip you with the essential terminology needed to successfully implement graphic novels as content-area texts. While we know that some of you might be familiar with the appropriate terminology involved in reading and teaching graphic novels, we feel that providing a sound, specific base for looking at graphic novels is necessary.

Graphic novels 101

Copy-friendly versions of these handouts can be found in the Appendix for use in your classrooms.

Panels. A graphic novel panel is a visual or implied boundary that contains a piece of the story (see Figure 2.1).

Figure 2.1: An example of a graphic novel panel from Vera Brosgol's Anya's Ghost (First Second Books, 2011)

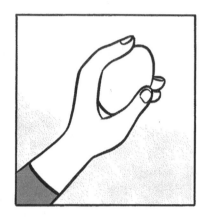

In this panel example, there is a visual, bold-lined boundary, and within that boundary, the reader learns that someone is holding an egg.

With the general idea of the panel understood, teachers and students can move on to the different types of graphic novel panels. There are eleven different types of graphic novel panels (see Figure 2.2.).

Figure 2.2: Eleven types of graphic novel panels, definitions, and examples

Type of Panel*	Definition	Example
Plot panel	Focuses on the action or events in the story	In these panels, readers get a solid idea of the plot. The main character, Anya, is struggling with her coming-of-age identity.

(continued)

Using Content-Area Graphic Texts for Learning

Type of Panel*	Definition	Example
Character panel	Focuses on the people, animals, and/or subjects of the story	In these three panels, the focus is on the characters of Anya and her little brother.
Setting panel	Focuses on where the story is taking place	In this panel, the focus is on the setting of the kitchen.
Conflict panel	Focuses on the tension in the story	These panels focus on the conflict between Anya's coming-of-age identity crisis and an unexpected source of help.
Rising action panel	Focuses on the events that escalate the tension in the story	These panels focus on the rising sense of insecurity Anya is having about her body image, especially compared to other girls.

(continued)

Chapter Two: Content-Area Graphic Novel Terminology 101

Type of Panel*	Definition	Example
Climax panel	Brings the rising action panels to a culminating moment or experience	In this panel, Anya confronts the ghost who really hasn't been a source of help for her identity crisis.
Resolution panel	Focuses on the solution to the tension and climax of the story	In these panels, Anya seems to have a more secure sense of self-respect and identity.
Symbols panel	Focuses on images or words that can stand for or represent more than one idea/thing in the story	These panels examine how closely Anya can relate to the ghost, a symbol for herself.

(continued)

Using Content-Area Graphic Texts for Learning

Type of Panel*	Definition	Example
Theme panel	Focuses on the main idea(s) of the story	In these panels, readers get a sense that one of Anya's main concerns is her body image.
Foreshadowing panel	Alludes to or insinuates something upcoming in the storyline	In these three panels, the reader learns a key piece of information: the ghost cannot be very far away from her bones.
Combination story panel	Combines two or more of the previously defined panels	In this panel, the focus is on two aspects of the story: the setting of the kitchen and the characterization of Anya's body image issues.

*Each panel example is from Vera Brosgol's *Anya's Ghost* (First Second Books, 2011).

Gutters. The gutter is the space in between the panels. In the gutter space, the reader integrates and transforms two ideas (from the adjoining panels) into a single idea; the panels come together to create a continuous, flowing story (Figure 2.3). There are six types of gutters (McCloud, 1993).

Figure 2.3: The six types of graphic novel gutters

Type of Gutter*	Definition	Example
Moment-to-moment gutter	Focuses on moving readers from one moment or instant in the story to the next moment or instant in the story	As Zita informs Joseph that she is pushing the big red button for his own good, the reader sees her from one moment (about to touch the button) to the next moment (touching the button).
Subject-to-subject gutter	Focuses first on one subject and then on another subject	In this gutter example, readers see one character/subject in the first panel and another character/subject in the second panel. From one panel, traveling through the gutter to the next panel, readers see two characters playing "chase."
Action-to-action gutter	An exciting gutter that moves readers from one action-packed moment to the next action-packed moment	This action-to-action gutter shows Zita as she is about to touch the mysterious red button and then, traveling through the gutter to the second panel, as she actually pushes the red button.

(continued)

Using Content-Area Graphic Texts for Learning

Type of Gutter*	Definition	Example
Aspect-to-aspect gutter	A gutter similar to tone or mood that pieces together a general feeling about the story	From one panel, through the gutter to the next panel and its gutter, and so on, readers get a sense of Zita's mood, which is nervous and scared.
Scene-to-scene gutter	Links various places and events in the story	In this gutter example, Zita is first shown in a few panels where she is captured by the Scriptorians. Moving through the gutter and into the last panel, the scene changes from Zita's scene to a new scene focused on Joseph as Zita sees that her friend is being held captive and hauled off to some sort of sacrificial ceremony.

(continued)

Type of Gutter*	Definition	Example
Non-sequitur gutter	Typically symbolic and links panels that have a deep, layered thematic meaning in the story; may seem nonsensical, but there is actually some rhyme and reason behind these gutters and their accompanying panels	In these panels and their gutters, readers see the same thing Zita and Joseph see: an unexplainable opening or crack in the air. Unexplainable to them and to the reader at the time, this gap turns into a thematic, transformational, and multi-dimensional opening that drives the plot.

* Each gutter example is taken from Ben Hatke's *Zita the Spacegirl* (First Second Books, 2010).

Balloons. Usually found inside a panel, balloons are the visual spaces where the print-text in the story appears (see Figure 2.4). There are six types of graphic novel balloons (Monnin, 2010, 2011).

Figure 2.4: The six types of graphic novel balloons

Type of Balloon*	Definition	
Staging balloons	Usually informational and set the stage for key elements of the story, such as plot, characterization, conflict, and/or setting	In this staging balloon, the author is describing a character and the year in which the story is going to begin.
Story balloons	Progress the storyline and move it along	In these creative-looking story balloons, the reader learns just how the main character sees the world of science.

(continued)

Using Content-Area Graphic Texts for Learning

Type of Balloon*	Definition	
Thought balloons	Reveal a character's thoughts (the reader will most likely feel like he or she is reading the character's mind)	In this example, Feynman is pondering the implications of making a new kind of bomb during World War II.
Dialogue balloons	Words based in conversation and said aloud by the characters	These dialogue balloons show the "fool physicist" speaking to his class.
Sound-effect balloons	Convey a sense of sound	In this sound-effect balloon, the reader hears the sound of the door slamming shut.
Balloon-less balloons	Evoke any of the five previously mentioned types of balloons, although not contained by any visual boundary; therefore, balloon-less balloons usually have two labels: balloon-less and one of the other five types	In these balloon-less balloons, which are also sound-effect balloons, the reader hears the characters laughing.

*Each panel example is from Jim Ottaviani's *Feynman* (First Second Books, 2011)

For your teaching convenience, the Appendix offers reproducible handouts of the key graphic novel terms: panels, gutters, and balloons. Knowing these terms will empower and enhance your specific content-area focus with graphic novels, as each term helps students to dive deeper into their reading experience with graphic novels.

Armed and empowered with graphic novel terminology 101, teachers and students are now ready to read a graphic novel. The second part of *Using Content-Area Graphic Texts for Learning* will build upon this graphic novel terminology and specifically link it to teaching content-area graphic novels in math, science, social studies, and language arts.

Teaching Content-Area Graphic Texts

In Part II, we enter each of the four content-area classrooms: math, language arts, social studies, and science. Within each of these content-area chapters, we discuss how graphic novels enhance the curriculum and help educators reach students with various learning strengths and needs. We also suggest content-area graphic novels for middle school use and provide lesson plans for integrating them into your classrooms. Each chapter will contain the following five basic elements:

✦ an overview of how graphic novels can help students tackle, integrate, and enhance content-area material;

✦ a graphic-novel-based content-area lesson plan;

✦ a demonstration of what that lesson plan is asking students to do, focusing on five learning skills—attention, memory, language, sequencing, and cognition—and how the lesson aligns with the appropriate content area's Common Core Standards;

✦ a discussion on how graphic novels help different types of learners succeed in the content-area classrooms; and

✦ a list of suggested graphic novels for each content-area classroom.

With this in mind, please meet our five students and their respective areas of strength and need.

Memory Megan has strong language and critical-thinking skills. She loves reading and writing poetry and always comes up with original ideas and perspectives. Her weaknesses are in memory. She has trouble keeping track of multi-step directions (active working memory) and remembering things she just read or heard (short-term memory), as well as recalling material previously memorized (long-term memory). Because she has strong spatial skills, she remembers things she sees and draws more easily than things she's heard or read. As a result, Megan has learned to draw simple illustrations, charts, and graphs in her notes to help her remember important facts, topics, and procedures.

Attention Andy remembers what he reads, hears, and learns and is always handing in creative work. His learning challenge lies in maintaining attention. Andy is easily distracted by outside noises, abrupt movement, and shiny objects. Furthermore, he has little patience for details, preferring to impulsively attack a task with limited planning and focus. As a result, he glosses over his work, often missing important content details and subtle nuances that directly affect a given narrative, task, or analysis. Andy, for example, often skims directions and impetuously "answers" math questions without writing out formulas or visually displaying his work. His writing is choppy because he does not focus on connecting thoughts or details, and editing written work is a challenge because he doesn't notice many of his errors. Andy is most successful when the learning tasks are broken into short bursts of activity.

Cognitive Coby has tremendous patience and is able to focus and work on a problem without distraction. His learning challenge is higher-order cognition. Coby has trouble thinking through problems, brainstorming, and quickly analyzing main ideas, themes, and patterns. His thinking is concrete, and he does not understand inferences. As a result, he can recall important aspects of a problem, but has difficulty deriving conclusions, solving abstract problems, or even coming up with original writing or ideas. He functions best when tasks and content are broken down into small, concrete, manageable segments and when he is given extra time to think things through.

Language Larry has a keen memory and great attention skills. His learning challenge is processing language. He experiences difficulties understanding what is said or read (receptive language), as well as relating his ideas when writing or speaking (expressive language). As a result, Larry finds it difficult to follow directions, read long or complex passages, and track lengthy class discussions. He also has trouble clearly relaying his ideas when writing or speaking. Preparing conversation bullets in advance allows Larry to participate in discussions, and smaller portions of text empower Larry to keep up when reading.

Sequential Sue has excellent language and comprehension skills. Her weaknesses lie in her ability to keep track of sequences. She is always late (can't keep track of time), can't remember dates, has a lot of trouble following multi-step instructions (especially those given verbally), and falls behind when asked to follow along or find an important passage in the reading. Sue also has trouble organizing her thoughts and materials and often comes to class unprepared. Keeping a schedule of classes available on her phone helps her keep track of where to be when, and she keeps written instructions for editing and math problem solving clearly available in the pocket folders of her notebooks.

Using Content-Area Graphic Texts for Learning

In these brief descriptions, we are sure you recognize these types of students within your own classrooms. We include these student learners in the following chapters to clearly illustrate their learning profiles and how graphic novels can be used to help address their learning needs. Before entering our content-area classrooms, however, it's critical that you look over Figure 3.1 on the following page.

Figure 3.1, on the following page, outlines how graphic novels can help each of these five students to be more successful content area readers and learners. In fact, we encourage you to copy and share this figure with your students to empower them to better understand their own learning strengths and needs. Hopefully, it will illuminate the role graphic novels can play in the classroom *and* help your students become more adept, critical readers of the content-area classroom graphic novels you will ask them to read.

Figure 3.1: How graphic novels can help the five student profiles

Graphic novel element	For weak memory learners	For weak attention learners	For weak cognitive learners	For weak language learners	For weak sequencing learners
Graphic novel panels provide multi-sensory means of attending, decoding, remembering, and sequencing information.	Condensed multi-sensory data makes the essential bits of information easier to identify, relate to, store, and remember.	Condensed multi-sensory data makes it easier to focus on and relate to text. Panels present the material in short bursts, making it easier to attend to.	Condensed multi-sensory data (where visual items support and enhance text), make the content easier to grasp, compare and contrast, and relate to.	Pairing condensed visual and verbal cues makes the text easier to comprehend, enabling and empowering weak language learners.	Panels make jumps in time, which require the reader to fill in the gaps and provide excellent sequencing practice opportunities.
Graphic novel gutters provide opportunities to pause, check comprehension, and construct what is happening in time and sequence between panels.	Natural pauses between panels allow students to stop, consolidate information, check comprehension, and store data.	Varying gaps of information between panels requires active focus and participation when reading.	Information gaps between panels requires active problem solving as readers construct what is missing.	Gutters allow weak language learners to pause and integrate the short verbal and visual text, making reading less daunting.	Gutter pauses allow readers to evaluate time sequences and integrate the story's natural sequence.
Graphic novel balloons focus the message into short manageable bits.	Short bits of text make information easier to store and retrieve.	Short bits of text make information easier to recognize, focus, and attend to.	Short bits of text make it easier for readers to recognize the main ideas.	Short bits of text allow for easier, faster processing of verbal input.	Short bits of text make following sequences of sentences and ideas less cumbersome.
Graphic novel art is inviting, engaging, and easy to relate to, as it reinforces and enhances the verbal message.	Attaching visual representations to people, events, and places helps create additional memory associations and paths.	Engaging art provides more stimulation than text alone, resulting in less need for outside stimulation or "mind trips."	Visual details help explain and reinforce content and abstract messages.	Visual details help weak language learners decipher the text and its meaning.	Visual sequences reinforce the verbal sequences, making them easier to follow and remember.
Graphic novel text is concise.	Concise text is easier to find when studying and entails smaller bits of data, making it easier to store and recall.	Concise text is easier to focus on and attend to.	Concise text removes excess "noise," making it easier to decipher the author's or character's intent.	Concise text is easier to decode.	Sequences of short bursts of text make it easier to follow a series of events throughout a time period.
Pairing of text and art reinforces the message, requires additional focus, and must be processed together as the reader constructs the author's message.	Visual details reinforce the text, making it easier to find and remember.	Readers must attend to small visual and verbal details, requiring more focus and attention, while being highly motivating.	Metaphors are rife in graphic novels, and the visual and verbal pairing makes them more obvious, more concrete, and easier to understand and relate to.	Advanced vocabulary paired with visual representations provides weak language learners exposure and opportunities to read, use, and comprehend advanced vocabulary.	Panels break the story into easily recognizable verbal and visual sequences, helping those weak in sequencing to recognize essential parts and sequences of stories, events, and data.

Graphic Novels in the Math Classroom

For some students, math is a lot of fun. It's a practical puzzle to be solved, and solutions tend to follow logical progressions. Others, however, find it abstract and too difficult to conceptualize. Some students love that there are no long texts to decode and no long papers to write, while others find word problems hard to decipher and solve ("If a train leaves New York at noon and is traveling at 50 miles per hour …"). Some just can't grasp what the problem is asking, while others find it easy to navigate the math problem and its "obvious" solution.

Everyone agrees, however, that the more personal and life-related the math problems are, the easier they are for students, regardless of their strengths and preferences, to follow. If lessons are made concrete and problems are related to students' personal lives, math becomes easier to grasp and recall. Integrating graphic novels into the math curriculum uniquely addresses these needs.

To help you integrate graphic novels into your math classrooms, this chapter presents:

1. An overview of how graphic novels can help different student learners tackle math material;

2. A specific, graphic novel-based math lesson plan;

3. A discussion of what the graphic novel math lesson is asking students to do—focusing on curriculum standards and five learning skills (attention, memory, language, sequencing, and cognition);

4. An alignment to the appropriate math Common Core Standards;

5. An illuminating discussion on how graphic novels will help five familiar yet different types of learners succeed in your math classrooms; and

6. A bibliography of suggested graphic novels for math classrooms.

How graphic novels can help students in math: a general overview

Graphic novels can be used in two very different ways in middle-school math:

1. They can be used as motivational tools to get students' attention while introducing and reinforcing math concepts.

2. They can be constructed/created to provide concrete, hands-on opportunities to reinforce concepts of geometry, ratios and proportional relationships, and measurement.

As there are two different ways to incorporate graphic novels into math classrooms, we present a lesson plan to illustrate each of these applications.

In our first lesson plan, we demonstrate how *Laika* by Nick Abadzis (First Second, 2007)—a story about Laika, the first sentient being flown into space by the Russians in the 1950s—can be used to help students understand how to construct and interpret ratios. In a sense, the graphic novel is being used as a motivational tool and a manipulative, much like blocks, wedges, or coins, while teaching math and strengthening language skills necessary in all classrooms and content areas.

In our second lesson plan, we demonstrate how, when making their own graphic novels, students integrate geometry, measurement, and proportional relationships as they design panels to express a creative story. This activity provides a concrete opportunity to examine the relationship between different shapes and space. It allows students to apply math concepts to real-life challenges, while reasoning abstractly and quantitatively. It also helps reinforce sequencing skills, attention to details, and expressive language skills. This lesson is especially helpful to teach and reinforce Common Core Standards in math.

Following each lesson plan, we will delineate the Common Core Standards addressed and the learning demands they place on students. The remainder of the chapter will discuss how each lesson addresses the learning needs of our five student types.

A math lesson using graphic novels as a math manipulative and motivational tool

Our first classroom visit will be with Ms. Fibonacci's fifth-grade math class. Her students are studying ratios, and many are having difficulty understanding the types of information ratios can "tell." To help her students better grasp the awesome power of ratios, Ms. Fibonacci has decided to use concrete examples that touch her students' everyday lives. She will use Nick Abadzis' graphic novel, *Laika* (First Second, 2007), to do so. She also wants to surprise them with what they may perceive as a cool and possibly unconventional math tool. Often classroom surprises—good ones—provide powerful learning experiences.

As the students enter the classroom, they notice copies of *Laika* on Ms. Fibonacci's desk. They know they're studying ratios in math and *Laika* in language arts, but this is math class! So, they are a bit confused. Why are their *Laika* books on Ms. Fibonacci's desk?

Goal: Continue working with ratios, emphasizing how they can be used and interpreted in meaningful ways.

Materials

- *Laika* by Nick Abadzis

- An empty, two-column table worksheet (Figure 3.2) to tabulate space versus Earth panels found in *Laika* to generate students' ratio. This ratio will be used to analyze whether the main story is more space- (science) or Earth- (socially/politically) related.

Class Activities

- Introduce and discuss *ratio*: why we use it and what it can tell us.
   - Optional point to think about: Did you know philosophers (Plato, Francis Bacon, Thomas Hobbes, John Locke, and Jean-Jacques Rousseau) routinely used the words *logos* (Greek meaning *logic*), *ratio*, and *reason* (*raison* in French) interchangeably. *Logos* was translated as a philosophical term into the Latin *ratio*. French then derived *raison* from the Latin *ratio*, and *raison* is considered the direct source of the English word, *reason*. You may want to map out this relationship (visually and verbally). Ask students why *ratio* and *reason* might have been used interchangeably. What do they have in common? (Note: You may not want to answer this immediately. Instead, pose the question, let students think about it while working, and answer in the closing class discussion.)

- Hand out worksheets (Figure 3.2, on page 29) and a copy of *Laika* to each student.

- Have students follow along as you read the worksheet directions.

- Discuss what might constitute Earth versus space panels. Record the class definitions on the board for students to refer to later when they will work independently.

- Using the book and the worksheet (Figure 3.2), review and tabulate the first few pages of *Laika* with the class. Refine the *Earth* and *space* definitions as necessary.
   - Look at page 5 in *Laika* (next page), for example. This is an interesting place to start your discussion of Earth and space, as the panels on this page are not clearly Earth or space, which will test and perhaps make the students tweak their definitions.
   - Now look at page 6 (next page), which shows a man battling the snow and asking a truck to "STOP! PLEASE!" These four panels are easily categorized as Earth.

Laika, Page 5   *Laika*, Page 6   *Laika*, Page 11

◇ One more page and example you may want to review with the class is page 11, which depicts a man looking up to the stars and moon in the first half of the panels. These panels will probably be categorized as space. In the final panels, the reader sees the man walking away, saying, "I'll find you somewhere warm," which relates to earthly issues.

✦ Important note: There will be disagreements with some panels. Don't get hung up on this discussion. The point right now is for each student to determine his or her own ratio of Earth to space. It is the process of tabulating and interpreting ratios that is important. If you want to, however, you can note these disagreements, which can lead to interesting discussions about averages, statistics, and standard deviations later.

✦ Discuss/demonstrate efficient ways students may record their data and keep track of the panels they have and have not recorded. They may, for example, want to color-code the columns (brown for Earth, blue for space), making it easier to recognize and locate the respective columns.

✦ Discuss how best to organize the tallies within each column to make it easier to tabulate the column totals. Students may, for example, want to have a separate line of tabulations for each page with the total for that page circled at the end of the line.

✦ Instruct students how to use the final "space" and "Earth" totals to construct their ratios.

✦ Students can work independently or in pairs. When finished, have them come together as a class for the closing discussion.

✦ Discuss what the ratio tells us. (In this case, inferring what was more important to this story: was this more a story about space or about social/political issues on Earth?)

Using Content-Area Graphic Texts for Learning

Figure 3.2: Space to Earth ratio worksheet

Space to Earth Ratio in *Laika*

Directions: You will be tabulating all the *Laika* panels in the columns below.

1. **Evaluate** each panel in the book, and decide if it is depicting a scene occurring on or related to land OR one occurring in or related to space.

2. **Enter your data:** When you evaluate each panel as space or Earth, enter a notch (short line), check mark, or "X" under the applicable column below.

3. **Add the entries:** After marking each panel under the "Earth" or "Space" column, add the total notches, check marks, or "Xs" in each column. Write these totals in the "Total" boxes under each column.

4. **Construct your ratio:** Take the total from the space column, and write it on the line above "Space" in the small center box toward the bottom of the sheet. Do the same thing for "Earth." This is your space to earth ratio.

5. **Reflect:** What do you think this ratio tells you? Write your response in the box at the bottom of the page.

Space	Earth
Total:	Total:

_____ _____
Space   Earth

What does this number tell you?

*See page 122 in the Appendix for a copy-friendly version of this handout.

- Ask students to brainstorm and consider what other ratios might tell us (e.g., the ratio of warm-color panels with red, yellow, and orange versus cold-color panels with blues, browns, blacks, and whites).

- **Optional discussion 1:** (relating to the lesson's introduction) Why did philosophers use the terms *reason* and *ratio* interchangeably?

- **Optional discussion 2:** (reviewing statistics) Record each student's (or student group's) ratio on the board. Discuss why these ratios may be different. (There may have been slightly different working definitions for *space* and *Earth*, or there may have been errors in students' computations. How do these differences affect the outcome? Compute a class average ratio. Discuss the information relayed by the average/mean and median.

The Laika lesson's demands

As you can see in Figure 3.3, this lesson addresses multiple Common Core math and reading standards that, in turn, demand multiple learning skills. This lesson requires students to process and understand the following Common Core standards in math:

- Ratios & Proportional Relationships: analyzing the book's space versus earth content

- The Number System: tabulating and adding the pace and Earth panels to generate ratios

- Measurement and Data: measuring and interpreting data

- Expressions and Equations: adding tallies, generating ratios, and analyzing what this ratio means

- Statistics and Probability: Determining the class's average ratio and summarizing and describing what the ratio distributions mean

Aside from these math standards, students must also process multiple Common Core language arts standards as they read, write, and communicate their thoughts and findings. We include these standards in Figure 3.3. While primarily teaching a lesson about ratios, Ms. Fibonacci also asked her students to identify key ideas and details, analyze data, and identify proportional relationships. To successfully meet these demands, students must rely on verbal and visual language processing, higher-order cognition, attention, memory, and sequencing of information within each required step of the assignment.

Language skills are necessary to decode Ms. Fibonacci's directions, class discussion, and what is written in each panel when determining space or Earth membership. These skills are also essential when students report their findings to the class and contribute to the class discussions.

Higher-order cognition skills are necessary for any type of analysis. In this lesson, students must understand the worksheet, Ms. Fibonacci's directions, and the distinction between space

and Earth panels. Students also use cognitive skills to compare and contrast panels, analyze what the derived ratio tells them, and follow, analyze and contribute to class discussions.

Attention skills are required to follow Ms. Fibonacci's directions and contributing to the discussions. Students must also attend to the panels' verbal and visual messages to determine whether they represent space or Earth. They must not skip or repeat coding the individual panels, and they must they enter their tallies in the correct columns, constantly keeping track of where they are.

Memory skills are necessary as students keep track of Ms. Fibonacci's directions and what constitutes space and Earth membership. Writing these distinctions on the board will help, but students have to remember to look at the board. When working on their ratio worksheets (Figure 3.2), students must remember their places, both in the book and on the worksheet, as they continue to record their data. Students must also remember what their ratio might tell when contributing to the class discussion. If Ms. Fibonacci decides to take a class average, students also must recall what "average" means and how to compute it.

Sequencing skills are necessary as students must follow the directions in the correct order, evaluate each of the panels in a given order, keep track of their tabulations by recording and tabulating them correctly, and follow the flow of the opening and closing class discussions.

Figure 3.3: What is Ms. Fibonacci asking her students to do?

Teacher's Instruction	Task Demands On Students	Skills Involved	Common Core Standards*
Hand out lesson materials; review directions.	✦ Read the directions. ✦ Focus on Ms. Fibonacci's review of the directions. ✦ Make sure they understand the directions. ✦ Keep track of their lesson materials.	✦ Attention – focusing on directions ✦ Language – decoding directions; following and interpreting the class discussions ✦ Cognition – understanding directions; evaluating how to best plan and meet lesson demands ✦ Sequencing and memory – remembering the order of steps	✦ Integration of Knowledge and Ideas (R/LA) ✦ Fluency (R/LA) ✦ Analyze Patterns and Relationships (M) ✦ Craft and Structure (R/LA) ✦ Key Ideas and Details (R/LA)
Discuss and define what constitutes an "Earth" versus "Space" panel.	✦ Follow (and ideally participate in) the class discussion. ✦ Read panel dialogues and narratives. ✦ Scrutinize illustrations. ✦ Define and evaluate panels to determine "Space" versus "Earth" membership.	✦ Attention – following class discussion; attending to text and illustration details to determine "Space" versus "Earth" membership ✦ Language – decoding what is read and said; defining "Space" versus "Earth" membership ✦ Cognition – analyzing verbal and visual patterns; determining group membership ✦ Memory – remembering what constitutes membership in "Space" versus "Earth" ✦ Sequencing – following the directions' steps	✦ Operations and Algebraic Thinking (M) ✦ Fluency (R/LA) ✦ Measurement and Data (M) ✦ Represent and Interpret Data (M) ✦ Craft and Structure (R/LA) ✦ Key Ideas and Details (/LA) ✦ Integration of Knowledge and Ideas (R/LA) ✦ Comprehension and Collaboration (R/LA) ✦ Presentation of Knowledge and Ideas (R/LA)

(continued)

Teacher's Instruction	Task Demands On Students	Skills Involved	Common Core Standards*
Students fill in the worksheet.	✦ Analyze the content of each panel to determine group membership. ✦ Make sure panels are not omitted or repeated. ✦ Compute totals for each group. ✦ Determine the ratio. ✦ Interpret the ratio.	✦ Attention – keeping track of where they are (in the book and on the worksheet); making sure nothing is omitted or repeated; focusing on and integrating verbal and visual cues to determine "Space" or "Earth" membership ✦ Language – decoding text to determine membership ✦ Cognition – analyzing patterns in verbal and visual information to determine group membership; analyzing what the ratio tells them ✦ Memory – remembering what constitutes membership in "Space" versus "Earth"; remembering what they just entered and what panel is next; remembering to complete all required steps ✦ Sequencing – keeping track of where they are in their tabulations; adding tallies correctly; following each step of the directions	✦ Range of Reading and Level of Text Complexity (R/LA) ✦ Fluency (R/LA) ✦ Represent and Interpret Data (M) ✦ Operations and Algebraic Thinking (M) ✦ Analyze Patterns and Relationships (M) ✦ Ratios and Proportional Relationships (M) ✦ Key Ideas and Details (R/LA) ✦ Compute Fluently with Multi-digit Numbers (M)
Class discussion: ✦ What do these ratios tell us? ✦ Why did students come up with different ratios?	✦ Read ratio correctly when reporting it to class ✦ Brainstorm what the ratio "tells" us ✦ Attend to and participate in class discussion ✦ Analyze/discuss why some ratios were different from others	✦ Attention – following class discussion; ensuring their ratio is reported correctly ✦ Language – reporting results accurately to the class; processing and contributing to class discussion ✦ Memory – remembering what their ratio might relay; recalling statistics if teacher follows discussion option #2 ✦ Cognition – evaluating class discussion; contributing insights to the discussion; analyzing why there may different ratios reported ✦ Sequencing – following the class discussion	✦ Compute Fluently with Multi-digit Numbers (M) ✦ Ratios and Proportional Relationships (M) ✦ Operations and Algebraic Thinking (M) ✦ Statistics and Probability (M) ✦ Develop Understanding of Statistical Variability ✦ Summarize and Describe Distributions ✦ Integration of Knowledge and Ideas (R/LA) ✦ Comprehension and Collaboration (R/LA) ✦ Presentation of Knowledge and Ideas (R/LA)

*NOTE: R/LA = Reading/Language Arts Common Core Standards; M = Math Common Core Standards

Constructing a graphic novel page lesson plan

Here is the second recommended lesson plan in geometry, which involves the construction of graphic novels.

Goal: Design a graphic novel page that contains five or more panels of at least two different geometric shapes.

Materials

✦ A selection of comics and graphic novels to look at and brainstorm from

✦ Geometry textbook or worksheet (Figure 3.4) with formulas for measuring and constructing circles, squares, rectangles, and pentagons

✦ Pencils

- ✦ Protractors
- ✦ Rulers
- ✦ Unlined paper

Class Activities

- ✦ Pass out a copy of Figure 3.4 on page 35 to each student and read the handout directions together.

- ✦ Review how to compute the area of the page, and then discuss how students might divide the page into at least five panels containing at least two different types of shapes. Give an example.

- ✦ Discuss how different shapes connote different ideas/concepts. For example, a pentagon may reflect characters stopping to do something; a circle may imply inclusion; a rectangle may provide a glimpse of a tall or long object (depending on how it is situated on the page); a square with wavy sides may represent a dream or flashback in time; and a triangle may represent a hierarchy.

- ✦ Brainstorm different types of page designs, showing them selected examples from various graphic novels.

- ✦ Allow students to independently look through a collection of graphic novels (either in class or in the school library), suggesting they make sketches of their favorite page designs.

- ✦ Hand three sheets of unlined paper to each student, reassuring them that there is more if they need it.

- ✦ Have students work independently on their graphic novel pages. Circulate among students to make sure they remain on task, answering questions when necessary.

- ✦ Debrief. Have students share their work when done.

The lesson demands of constructing a graphic novel

As you can see, this lesson constructing a graphic novel page is very different from the first lesson incorporating an existing graphic novel (*Laika*) into your curriculum. It, therefore, has its own learning demands while addressing similar Common Core Standards.

As indicated in Figure 3.5, this lesson addresses multiple Common Core Standards in both math and reading that, in turn, demand multiple learning skills. This lesson requires students to process and understand the following core standards in math:

- ✦ Ratios and proportional relationships – as they calculate how to incorporate the different panel sizes and shapes onto a page

- The number system – as they calculate how to set up their panels on the page

- Measurement and data – as they measure and draw their five panels (consisting of at least two different shapes)

- Expressions and equations – as they apply geometry equations dividing the area of the page into five panels of at least two different shapes

Aside from these math standards, students must also process multiple Common Core language arts standards as they read the directions and write their stories. We include these standards in Figure 3.5. While primarily teaching a lesson in geometry, Ms. Fibonacci is also asking her students to identify key ideas and details, craft and structure a one-page story, integrate knowledge and ideas, and identify proportional relationships. To successfully meet these demands, students must rely on verbal and visual language processing, memory, attention, higher-order cognition, and the sequencing of information within each required step of the assignment.

Language skills are necessary to decode Ms. Fibonacci's directions, to read and evaluate the different geometry formulas, and to follow and contribute to class discussion. They are also essential to construct one-page stories and to break the story into five sequential panels.

Higher-order cognition skills are necessary for any type of analysis. In this lesson, they are employed to understand Ms. Fibonacci's directions, to brainstorm how to most efficiently divide the page into five panels, and to create an interesting, comprehensible one-page story. Students will also have to figure out the size of the panels, how to illustrate their panels, and what colors to employ to best relay the story's desired emotions and intent.

Attention skills are essential as students focus on Ms. Fibonacci's directions and class discussions. Aside from attending and contributing to discussions, students must continuously focus and monitor their work, making sure their five panels tell a story that makes sense. They also have to focus on details of their calculations to efficiently and aesthetically set up their panels in a meaningful and appealing manner.

Memory skills are necessary for students to remember and follow Ms. Fibonacci's directions. Students will also have to remember how to determine the area of the page, divide the area into five panels, and construct at least two different-shaped panels. Students will also have to remember what they want to say and how they want to illustrate it.

Sequencing skills are essential for students to follow the discussion trends as well as to complete directions in the correct order. Students first have to break a story into verbal and visual parts. They must then determine the area of the page and figure out how to divide it into five panels. When deconstructing the story into five parts, students have to make sure the parts flow and make sense and that the panel placements aid the story's sequence. If a sequence is omitted, it will clearly affect the final product.

Using Content-Area Graphic Texts for Learning

Instructions for Designing a Graphic Novel Page

Design a page for a graphic novel with at least five panels. These panels must take up the entire area of the page, making it easier to read and more pleasing to the eye. The five (or more) panels on this page must consist of two or more different shapes. These panels may be circles, rectangles, squares, and/or pentagons.

Formula reminders

A circle's area = pi x radius squared (or πr2)

A square's area = base x height

A rectangle's area = base x height

A triangle's area = 1/2 x base x height

A pentagon's area = the area of a triangle + the area of a rectangle

Page design directions

✦ Write a story in which the number of sentences or story parts equals the number of panels you want to use on your page. This will determine how many panels you will have on the page. (Note that your page must contain at least five panels.)

✦ Determine the area of the page.

✦ Divide the area of the page into the number of panels you intend to make. This number will represent the area of each shaped panel.

✦ Decide which shapes (at least two different types) you want to include on the page and how you want them distributed on the page. Note that different shapes can connote different ideas or impressions. Use these shapes to help emphasize and tell your story.

✦ Draw each of your panels.

✦ Write and illustrate a story to fit in the panels. Use different colors, fonts, and panel shapes to help emphasize points of your story.

*See page 123 in the Appendix for a copy-friendly version of this handout.

Figure 3.5: What is involved in constructing graphic novels?

Teacher's Instruction	Task Demands On Students	Skills Involved	Common Core Standards*
Write a short five-sentence story.	✦ Focus on the directions. ✦ Brainstorm story ideas. ✦ Deconstruct their story into five sequential parts. ✦ Make sure the sequences of the story make sense.	✦ Attention – focusing on directions while brainstorming ideas; making sure the story's segments flow and make sense ✦ Language – decoding directions; creating five comprehensible story segments ✦ Cognition – understanding directions; evaluating how to best plan and meet lesson demands; brainstorming ideas to write about; ensuring the story segments make sense ✦ Memory – keeping the story details in mind as it is being written and illustrated ✦ Sequencing and memory – remembering and following directions in the correct order; and deconstructing the story into five comprehensible segments	✦ Integration of Knowledge and Ideas (R/LA) ✦ Craft and Structure (R/LA) ✦ Key Ideas and Details (R/LA) ✦ Text Types and Purposes (R/LA) ✦ Production and Distribution of Writing (R/LA)Range of Writing (R/LA)

Determine the area of a page of paper.	✦ Attend to formulas on the worksheet.
	✦ Discriminate among and decide which formulas are most appropriate to determine the area of the page.
		✦ Attention – determining appropriate shape formula for area and focusing on its computation; monitoring progress of work
		✦ Language – reading and following the worksheet; decoding the formula for area
		✦ Cognition – understanding how to compute area
		✦ Memory – remembering which formulas best apply
		✦ Sequencing – making sure the formula is computed in the correct order
			✦ Operations and Algebraic Thinking (M)
			  ◇ Write and interpret numerical expressions.
			✦ Geometry (M)
			  ◇ Solve real-world and mathematical problems.
			✦ Measurement and Data (M)
			✦ Craft and Structure (R/LA)
			✦ Key Ideas and Details (R/LA)
			✦ Integration of Knowledge and Ideas (R/LA)

Divide the area of the page into five (or more) panels, and construct the five panels so they fit the page.	✦ Understand the necessary sequence of steps to compute the area for the shapes selected.
	✦ Brainstorm how best to organize the five panels as they fill the page.
	✦ Ensure there are at least two different-shaped panels on the page.
		✦ Attention – attending and processing; making sure the panels fit properly on the page; making sure the correct formula is applied; monitoring work to make sure the shapes and their placement are correct
		✦ Language – following written and oral directions; following the correct math formulas
		✦ Cognition – brainstorming how best to organize the page; understanding how to compute the appropriate formulas
		✦ Memory – remembering which formulas to use; remembering to complete all required steps
		✦ Sequencing – keeping track of panels and tabulations; remembering to follow each step of the directions in the correct order
			✦ Operations and Algebraic Thinking (M)
			  ◇ Write and interpret numerical expressions.
			✦ Geometry (M)
			  ◇ Solve real-world and mathematical problems.
			  ◇ Draw construct, and describe geometrical figures and describe relationships between them.
			✦ Measurement and Data (M)
			✦ Geometric Measurement: Understand Concepts of Volume (M)
			✦ Analyze Patterns and Relationships (M)
			✦ Integration of Knowledge and Ideas (R/LA)
			✦ The Number System (M)

(continued)

Teacher's Instruction	Task Demands On Students	Skills Involved	Common Core Standards*
Draw each panel	✦ Remember which shaped panels to use and where they should be placed on the page; remember which formulas to use for the selected shapes. ✦ Ensure the formulas are executed appropriately and the panels fit.	✦ Memory – recalling which shapes to use; remembering which formulas correspond to the selected shapes ✦ Attention – focusing on the details of each formula; ensuring formulas are executed correctly ✦ Sequencing – making sure each step of the formula is computed in the correct order; making sure the panels follow the correct order ✦ Cognition – evaluating progress as the page develops; and brainstorming how to adapt and adjust the panel arrangement if it does not come out as expected ✦ Language – following directions	✦ Operations and Algebraic Thinking (M) ◇ Write and interpret numerical expressions. ✦ Geometry (M) ◇ Solve real-world and mathematical problems ◇ Draw construct, and describe geometrical figures and describe relationships between them. ✦ Measurement and Data (M) ✦ Geometric Measurement: Understand Concepts of Volume (M) ✦ Analyze Patterns and Relationships (M) ✦ Integration of Knowledge and Ideas (R/LA) ✦ The Number System (M)
Write and illustrate the story to fit in the panels.	✦ Relay the story so that it is clearly written and easily followed. ✦ Make sure illustrations correspond to the correct text box. ✦ Select the right font size and shape so the text fits in the panel. ✦ Draw enough appropriate detail in the illustration so the image enhances and corresponds to the text. ✦ Make sure the panels follow the correct sequence so the story makes sense.	✦ Language – making sure the text makes sense, is easily understood, and fits in the appropriate text boxes ✦ Attention to detail – ensuring illustrations and text match, the story makes sense, and the text fits in the text boxes ✦ Memory – remembering what to put where ✦ Sequencing – making sure the text, illustrations, and panels are in the correct sequence so they fit together to tell the story ✦ Cognition – creating illustrations that enhance the text and show intent and emotions not included in the text; brainstorming which fonts best relate the text and fit in the text boxes; brainstorming how to adjust the text to fit the panels if necessary	✦ Craft and Structure (R/LA) ✦ Key Ideas and Details (R/LA) ✦ Analyze Patterns and Relationships (M) ✦ Integration of Knowledge and Ideas (R/LA) ✦ Range of Reading and Level of Text Complexity (R/LA) ✦ Text Types and Purposes (R/LA) ✦ Production and Distribution of Writing (R/LA) ✦ Range of Writing (R/LA) ✦ Presentation of Knowledge and Ideas (R/LA)

*Note: R/LA = Reading/Language Arts Common Core Standards; M = Math Common Core Standards

How graphic novels help our five students in math

Memory Megan: Megan has weak memory skills. Typically in math, students like Megan exhibit trouble remembering which formulas to use when and often cannot recall instructional directions. As graphic novels pair visual and verbal information, this pairing establishes additional memory associations, making it easier to store and retrieve information.

In our first lesson plan, we ask students to determine the ratio of panels containing content about space exploration and those that relate to social interactions and events on Earth. When determining the graphic novel's space:Earth ratio, students are calculating a visual/ verbal ratio. They are effectively creating multiple memory paths for ratio—a visual memory path (by comparing and contrasting illustration details), a verbal memory path (by analyzing and contrasting the written content), and even a tactile memory path (as they tabulate the ratio). This multi-sensory approach provides students like Megan additional means and opportunities to associate, chunk, and remember how to construct and interpret ratio. The fact that the ratio lesson helps identify a dominant theme in *Laika* will help Megan remember the book's main idea in her language arts class.

In our second graphic novel application, creating a graphic novel page provides students like Megan hands-on opportunities to reinforce concepts and formulas in geometry. Designing a graphic novel page by dividing its area into various shaped panels reinforces geometry formulas, pattern recognition, proportional relationships, measurement, and operational skills. It also provides multi-sensory memory paths for learning and storing data, while empowering students to integrate stories and topics they love into their classroom learning experiences.

Attention Andy has difficulty sustaining his focus and attention. Typically in math, students like Andy find it difficult to focus on details, and impulsively figure out math problems, often neglecting subtle but important aspects of the problem. Graphic novels provide a wonderful medium for children with attention issues, because they relay information in short verbal and visual bursts. Graphic novels also force readers to slow down as they attend to and integrate the illustration and text details. Furthermore, the panels are entertaining and the art inviting, making it easier to focus on, integrate, and evaluate content.

In our first lesson plan, when determining space: Earth ratios, our students have to focus on short bursts of visual and verbal details in the panels as well as on details when tabulating the ratios. Furthermore, when evaluating the panels, students construct short, concrete panel summaries illuminating the author's message and intent while providing insight and experience with constructing and interpreting "ratio."

In our second lesson plan, constructing a graphic novel page requires students like Andy to slow down and focus on details as well. For one thing, students have to focus on accurate measurements when creating panel shapes. They must also focus on how to divide the story into panels, how to divide the area of a given page into panels, and how to arrange the panels on the page. In addition to focusing on construction details, this lesson also reinforces attending concepts in geometry, operations, measurement, and proportional relationships, while requiring students to succinctly relay a story. Furthermore, as this is only a five-panel story, the work reinforces shorter bursts of visual/verbal/mental focus.

Cognitive Coby is weak with critical thinking, analysis, and brainstorming. Typically, students like Coby have trouble comparing and contrasting, recognizing patterns, and making and interpreting inferences. Math provides a particular challenge for these students, because so much of the content is abstract and involves some sort of analysis and pattern recognition.

The concrete act of constructing a ratio in our first lesson helps students like Coby more fully comprehend what is involved in constructing and interpreting ratios. The vibrant, visual component of graphic novels helps delineate and clarify ideas. Furthermore, interpreting the ratio he constructs not only helps Coby understand what a ratio can tell, but also helps him grasp *Laika*'s main idea.

In our second lesson, constructing a graphic novel provides students like Coby with hands-on opportunities using specific formulas to construct geometric shapes while deconstructing a short story. Coby must refine the story's main ideas, brainstorm page and panel design, and determine how to use the art to enhance and detail his story. Constructing panels of various shapes and sizes also provides students with concrete and meaningful exercises that help them understand, integrate, and reinforce concepts of proportional relationships, measurement, operations, pattern recognition, and geometry.

Language Larry has difficulty interpreting what he reads and hears (receptive language) and explaining his ideas when he speaks and writes (expressive language). Graphic novels are an excellent language and learning tool for students like Larry, because the visual component supports, reinforces, and further develops the verbal message. Furthermore, the verbal content is presented in short bursts that are less daunting for weak language learners. In math, even though numbers are involved, much of the instruction is verbal. Hands-on opportunities in math are essential for weak language learners.

In our ratio lesson, students can check verbal comprehension with the accompanying illustrations. This lesson also reinforces the steps necessary for constructing ratio and provides a concrete visual component (looking at the illustrations) and tactile component (recording the data) that help weak language learners integrate and better understand the steps needed to build and interpret ratios.

Our second lesson plan, constructing a graphic novel, provides students like Larry with opportunities to integrate mathematical equations, art, and concise language to develop and relay a story. They must then navigate formulas to physically set up the page and its story. Deconstructing the story into short verbal and visual components provides students greater insight into a story's dynamics. Designing a graphic novel page also empowers students to integrate text and geometry while reinforcing proportional relationships, measurement, and operation skills to create a verbal-visual story.

Sequential Sue has difficulty remembering and following sequences. Math is all about following sequences of steps breaking down problems, applying formulas, and building solutions. Graphic novels provide sequencing practice for Sue, because she must follow the verbal, visual and temporal (time related) sequences in graphic novels.

In our ratio-building lesson below, Sue must code sequences of panels while following the required steps to calculate ratio. This provides her with concrete, hands-on experiences decoding visual and verbal sequences. The fact that Sue likes graphic novels makes a potentially daunting task of tracking and recording each panel more fun and meaningful. This multi-sensory hands-on approach also provides additional means and opportunities to associate, chunk, and remember the steps involved in constructing and interpreting ratios.

Our second lesson (constructing a graphic novel) provides multiple opportunities to evaluate sequence as well. Students first have to break their stories into verbal and visual sequences. They must then follow the necessary steps and operational procedures to divide the area of a page into a given number of shapes, and follow another sequence of steps to create the desired shaped panels. Throughout this exercise, students must focus on verbal and visual content, measurement, mathematical operations, and proportional relationships.

Conclusion and suggested graphic novels for middle-school math instruction

Whether they are used to motivate, introduce, or reinforce math content in the classroom, graphic novels clearly have a place in middle-school math instruction. They integrate Common Core Standards in math and reading while appealing to students with varying skills and affinities.

Just as our students have diverse learning styles and preferences, we, as teachers, have our own teaching styles and preferences, and our schools often have different teaching and curricular guidelines. To meet these varying needs and affinities, we provide you with a list of appropriate graphic novels you may want to consider integrating into your classrooms. In the following list, we present some of our favorite titles along with suggested reading grade levels and the math and reading Common Core Standards these books address.

Figure 3.6: A middle-level cross-index of thematically identified and standards-aligned math graphic novels

Title and Author	Grade Level	Math Standards	Reading Standards

The 9/11 Report: A Graphic Adaptation by Sid Jacobson and Ernie Colón	6–8	✦ Represent and Interpret Data
		✦ Analyze patterns and relationships
		✦ Operations and Algebraic
		✦ Compute fluently with multidigit numbers
		✦ Statistics and Probability
		  ◇ Develop understanding of statistical variability
		  ◇ Summarize and describe distributions
		✦ The Number System
			✦ Key Ideas and Details
			✦ Craft and Structure
			✦ Integration of Knowledge and Ideas
			✦ Fluency
			✦ Range of Reading and Level of Text Complexity
			✦ Text Types and Purposes

(continued)

Title and Author	Grade Level	Math Standards	Reading Standards
Big Fat Little Lit, edited by Art Spiegelman and Françoise Mouly	4–8	✦ Measurement and Data ✦ Geometry ✦ Ratios and Proportional Relationships	✦ Key Ideas and Details ✦ Craft and Structure ✦ Integration of Knowledge and Ideas ✦ Fluency ✦ Range of Reading and Level of Text Complexity ✦ Text Types and Purposes
Flight: Volume One, edited by Kazu Kibuishi*	6–8	✦ Ratios and Proportional Relationships ✦ Statistics and Probability	✦ Key Ideas and Details ✦ Craft and Structure ✦ Integration of Knowledge and Ideas ✦ Fluency ✦ Range of Reading and Level of Text Complexity ✦ Text Types and Purposes
G-Man Vol. 1: Learning to Fly by Chris Giarrusso*	4–6	✦ Measurement and Data ✦ Geometry	✦ Key Ideas and Details ✦ Craft and Structure ✦ Integration of Knowledge and Ideas ✦ Fluency ✦ Range of Reading and Level of Text Complexity ✦ Text Types and Purposes
Gigantic by Rick Remender	6–8	✦ Ratios and Proportional Relationships ✦ Number System ✦ Geometry ✦ Statistics and Probability	✦ Key Ideas and Details ✦ Craft and Structure ✦ Integration of Knowledge and Ideas ✦ Fluency ✦ Range of Reading and Level of Text Complexity ✦ Text Types and Purposes
Lex Luthor: Man of Steel by Brian Azzarello and Lee Bermejo	6–8	✦ Ratios and Proportional Relationships ✦ Number System ✦ Geometry ✦ Statistics and Probability	✦ Key Ideas and Details ✦ Craft and Structure ✦ Integration of Knowledge and Ideas ✦ Fluency ✦ Range of Reading and Level of Text Complexity ✦ Text Types and Purposes
Plastic Man: On the Lam by Kyle Baker*	5–8	✦ Measurement and Data ✦ Geometry ✦ Ratios and ✦ Proportional Relationships ✦ Functions	✦ Key Ideas and Details ✦ Craft and Structure ✦ Integration of Knowledge and Ideas ✦ Fluency ✦ Range of Reading and Level of Text Complexity ✦ Text Types and Purposes
Sherlock Holmes, Vol. 1: The Trial of Sherlock Holmes by Leah Moore, John Reppion, and Aaron Campbell*	6–8	✦ Geometry ✦ Statistics and Probability ✦ Ratios and Proportional Relationships ✦ Measurement and Data	✦ Key Ideas and Details ✦ Craft and Structure ✦ Integration of Knowledge and Ideas ✦ Fluency ✦ Range of Reading and Level of Text Complexity ✦ Text Types and Purposes

(continued)

Title and Author	Grade Level	Math Standards	Reading Standards
Star Wars: Clone Wars Adventures, Vol. 1 by Haden Blackman, Matt Fillbach, Shawn Fillbach, and Ben Caldwell*	4–6	✦ Ratios and Proportional Relationships ✦ Number System ✦ Geometry ✦ Statistics and Probability ✦ Measurement and Data	✦ Key Ideas and Details ✦ Craft and Structure ✦ Integration of Knowledge and Ideas ✦ Fluency ✦ Range of Reading and Level of Text Complexity ✦ Text Types and Purposes
Superman: Red Son by Mark Millar, David Johnson, Kilian Plunkett, Andrew Robinson, and Walden Wong	6–8	✦ Ratios and Proportional Relationships ✦ Number System ✦ Geometry ✦ Statistics and Probability	✦ Key Ideas and Details ✦ Craft and Structure ✦ Integration of Knowledge and Ideas ✦ Fluency ✦ Range of Reading and Level of Text Complexity ✦ Text Types and Purposes
Treasure Island by Robert Louis Stevenson, adapted by Andrew Harrar and Richard Kohlrus	6–8	✦ Number System ✦ Geometry ✦ Analyze patterns and relationships	✦ Key Ideas and Details ✦ Craft and Structure ✦ Integration of Knowledge and Ideas ✦ Fluency ✦ Range of Reading and Level of Text Complexity ✦ Text Types and Purposes

* This graphic novel is part of a series.

Graphic Novels in the Language Arts Classroom

Graphic novels lend themselves to the language arts curriculum. They engage all types of language learners, addressing both visual and verbal literacy skills. They are particularly helpful for weak language learners, as graphic novels enable these students to rely on visual and graphic cues as well as verbal and language cues. Furthermore, graphic novels are engaging, pertinent, and motivating, and the vastly expanding number of high-quality, content-area graphic novels make their integration into middle-school language arts classes an easy, natural extension of modern culture.

To help you integrate graphic novels into your language arts classrooms, this chapter presents:

1. An overview of how graphic novels can help different student learners tackle language arts material;

2. A specific, graphic novel-based language arts lesson plan;

3. A discussion of what the graphic novel language arts lesson is asking students to do—focusing on five learning skills (attention, memory, language, sequencing, and cognition);

4. An alignment to the appropriate language arts Common Core Standards;

5. An illuminating discussion on how graphic novels will help five familiar yet different types of learners succeed in your language arts classrooms; and

6. A lengthy bibliography of suggested graphic novels for language arts classrooms.

How graphic novels can help students in language arts: a general overview

Language arts teachers interested in teaching content-area graphic novels are extremely fortunate. There are hundreds of graphic novels available for middle-level language arts. Although we wish we could highlight all of these graphic novels in this chapter, we will highlight one, high-quality graphic novel in particular: Eisner-winning *Smile* (2010) by *The New York Times* bestselling author Raina Telgemeier. We will also present two lesson plans: one for teaching reading with *Smile,* alongside a traditional print-text novel (*The Outsiders* by S.E. Hinton) and the other for teaching writing with *Americus* by MK Reed and Jonathan Hill. Copy-friendly handouts for both lesson plans are in the Appendix on pages 124–131.

Because there are so many high-quality and age-appropriate language arts graphic novels available, there are a number of advantages to adopting them as classroom texts. Based on the standards set forth by The International Reading Association (IRA) and the National Council of Teachers of English (NCTE), the three most important reasons for adopting language arts graphic novels run parallel to both our reading and writing lesson plans, each of which will also include English language learning (ELL) enrichment ideas:

1. Language arts-based graphic novels reinforce the international and national standards for teaching reading in contemporary language arts classrooms;

2. They reinforce the international and national standards for teaching writing in contemporary language arts classrooms; and

3. They reach out to English language learners (ELLs) and address the international and national standards for teaching ELLs in language arts classrooms.

With these advantages in mind, take a look at Mr. Merlin's lessons for reading and writing.

Teaching reading with middle-level language arts graphic novels

Mr. Merlin's language arts classroom is full of books—all kinds of books. Poetry, fiction, nonfiction, magazines, newspapers, brochures, travel logs, and many more genres and formats take up every square inch of bookshelf space. In fact, his students are notorious for telling their parents and teachers that Mr. Merlin's classroom feels like a mystical library full of opportunities, like the floor-to-ceiling library in the Disney version of *Beauty and the Beast*. But books and paper texts are not the only sources of literacy learning in Mr. Merlin's classroom. Computer, iPod, and interactive whiteboard stations are found in his classroom as well. And, according to his students, Mr. Merlin's vast definition of what counts as literacy means he "really gets it." More and more in tune with a modern definition and understanding of teaching literacy (reading and writing), Mr. Merlin's language arts classroom is representative of all the various types of literacies students encounter on a daily basis in and out of school (Kist, 2004, 2009). In his classroom, traditional print-text literacies share the stage with more modern, visually-based literacies.

Some of Mr. Merlin's favorite books, those that provide the strongest links between teaching traditional print-text literacies and the more visually dominant literacies, are also perhaps

the most engaging books. Mr. Merlin is a graphic novel guru. He has an entire bookcase of middle-level graphic novels in the front of the room, right next to his desk; for your teaching convenience, you can find a bibliographical reference list of Mr. Merlin's graphic novel bookshelf at the end of this chapter.

But today, as Mr. Merlin's students enter his classroom, a space where print-text literacies and visual literacies share the stage, his students find both a graphic novel and a traditional print-text novel on each of their desks: *Smile* by Raina Telgemeier and *The Outsiders* by S.E. Hinton.

Invited by Mr. Merlin to observe how he teaches graphic novels alongside traditional, print-text literature over the next couple of days, we find ourselves seated in the back of the classroom. He begins his reading-centered lesson plan by explaining how today's language arts teachers must equally value imaged-based literacies, like those found in graphic novels, and traditional print-text literacies.

Identifying the elements of story in both a traditional, print-text novel and a contemporary graphic novel

Goal: Students will read and identify and discuss the elements of story in a traditional print-text novel and a graphic novel.

Materials

◆ *Smile* by Raina Telgemeier and *The Outsiders* by S.E. Hinton[1]

◆ Two blank worksheets (Figure 4.1, page 46) for "The Literate Eye" (Monnin, 2010) activity

Class Activities

1. Hand out, introduce, and discuss the elements of story found on the "Literate Eye" worksheet (Figure 4.1). Ask students to brainstorm or suggest definitions for each element of story. Keep student ideas on the board.

2. Sometimes it is helpful for middle-level students to understand and explain how the IRA/NCTE standards for teaching middle-level language arts directly relate to reading traditional, print-text literature alongside contemporary graphic novel literature in modern ELA classrooms. To do so, middle-level teachers may want to note and discuss the dualistic traditional and contemporary emphases found in the following IRA/NCTE standards:

---

[1] In case *The Outsiders* is too advanced for your middle-level students, we recommend the following two literary alternatives: *Holes* by Louis Sachar or *Diary of a Wimpy Kid* by Jeff Kinney.

Figure 4.1: "The Literate Eye" *

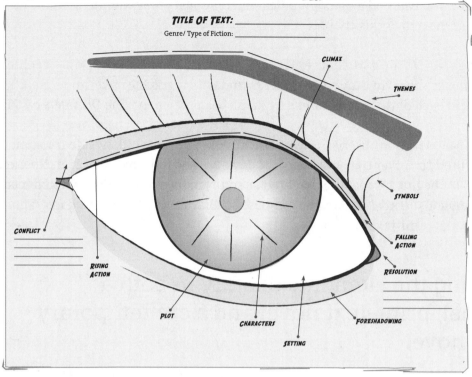

THE LITERATE EYE READING STRATEGY FOR MIDDLE SCHOOL ELA STUDENTS

TITLE OF TEXT: _____

Genre/ Type of Fiction: _____

CLIMAX

THEMES

CONFLICT

RISING ACTION

PLOT

CHARACTERS

SETTING

FORESHADOWING

SYMBOLS

FALLING ACTION

RESOLUTION

THE LITERATE EYE READING STRATEGY FOR MIDDLE SCHOOL ELA STUDENTS

Below each term, in the space on the right, please rewrite this term and its definition in your own words. In the space on the left, please illustrate your definition.

PLOT — the primary sequence of events that setup or tell a story

YOUR ILLUSTRATION	YOUR WORDS

CHARACTER — a person, persona, or identity within a fiction story

YOUR ILLUSTRATION	YOUR WORDS

SETTING — where the events of the story take place

YOUR ILLUSTRATION	YOUR WORDS

CONFLICT — the tension, disagreement, or discord that occurs in a story

YOUR ILLUSTRATION	YOUR WORDS

RISING ACTION — the action or events in the story that stem from the primary conflict and lead to the climax

YOUR ILLUSTRATION	YOUR WORDS

CLIMAX — the point of greatest intensity in a story, a culminating point, usually led up to by rising action and followed by a resolution

YOUR ILLUSTRATION	YOUR WORDS

RESOLUTION — the final outcome to solve or address the conflict

YOUR ILLUSTRATION	YOUR WORDS

SYMBOLS — an iconic representation that stands for something larger than itself

YOUR ILLUSTRATION	YOUR WORDS

THEME — a main idea or emphasized aspect of a story

YOUR ILLUSTRATION	YOUR WORDS

FORESHADOWING — a moment in the story when the reader feels like something to happen later in the story is alluded to or referenced

YOUR ILLUSTRATION	YOUR WORDS

*See Appendix pages 124–126 for full-size handouts.

Using Content-Area Graphic Texts for Learning

a. IRA/NCTE Standard 1: "Students read a wide range of print and non-print texts to build an understanding of texts, of themselves, and of the cultures of the United States and the world; to acquire new information; to respond to the needs and demands of society and the workplace; and for personal fulfillment. Among these texts are fiction and nonfiction, classic and contemporary works."

b. IRA/NCTE Standard 2: "Students read a wide range of literature from many periods in many genres to build an understanding of the many dimensions (e.g., philosophical, ethical, aesthetic) of human experience."

c. IRA/NCTE Standard 3: "Students apply a wide range of strategies to comprehend, interpret, evaluate, and appreciate texts. They draw on their prior experience, their interactions with other readers and writers, their knowledge of word meaning and of other texts, their word identification strategies, and their understanding of textual features (e.g., sound-letter correspondence, sentence structure, context, graphics)."

3. Following the class's discussion of the "Literate Eye," emphasizing the elements of story and the first three IRA/NCTE standards, teachers should divide the classroom into groups.

4. After forming these groups, teachers can ask them to take a quick book walk through S.E. Hinton's *The Outsiders* and through Raina Telgemeier's *Smile*. After students look through the books for 15–20 minutes, teachers should draw two columns on the board and call upon students to share their book walk predictions for each text.

Book Walk Predictions for The *Outsiders*	Book Walk Predictions for *Smile*

5. After discussing student predictions for *The Outsiders* and *Smile*, it is time to start reading the two texts. To optimize student understanding of each text and its elements of story, give each group a number. The even-numbered groups will begin reading *The Outsiders*, and the odd-numbered groups will read *Smile*.

Note: The following two-week schedule outlines how language arts teachers may want to organize their time. However, many schools follow various schedules. Please feel free to adapt this two-week schedule to your school's agenda.

Suggested Reading Schedule for *The Outsiders* and *Smile*
Week 1 **Day 1:** Students read the first quarter of their initial text **Day 2:** Students read the second quarter of their initial text **Day 3:** Students read the third quarter of their initial text **Day 4:** Students read the final quarter of their initial text **Day 5:** Team students with a peer who has read the opposite book that week, and ask the pair to explain the elements of story on their "Literate Eye" handouts to each other.
Week 2 **Day 1:** Students read the first quarter of their second text **Day 2:** Students read the second quarter of their second text **Day 3:** Students read the third quarter of their second text **Day 4:** Students read the final quarter of their second text **Day 5:** Team students with a peer who has read the opposite book that week, and ask the pair to explain the elements of story on their "Literate Eye" handouts to each other.

6. During each class meeting, teachers can divide their instruction time into three key steps:

   a. Step 1: 5–10 minutes for students to pair up with someone who has read the opposite text and share and/or update each other on that day's assigned reading

   b. Step 2: 20–30 minutes to read the next portion of text, due the following day (the remainder of that day's reading is considered homework) OR, for comprehension and assessment's sake, teachers can help students in their daily conversations by providing a graphic organizer that focuses on one or more elements of story (a character map, a plot timeline, a thematic table, an illustrated setting, etc.)

   c. Step 3: 10–15 minutes for students to add new information to their "Literate Eye" handouts (students should also feel free to add to their handouts while reading for homework)

7. For assessment purposes, we suggest teachers ask students to turn in their "Literate Eye" handouts for each text, as well as any other graphic organizers.

8. ELL enrichment opportunity: To enhance this opportunity for English language learners, teachers can prepare thematic reading assignment handouts by copying key panels that focus on the theme(s) appropriate for that day. At the beginning of each day, teachers will present ELLs with these handouts, which have a two-fold purpose: a) to stimulate student understanding of the major themes found in each assigned text and b) to provide visual reinforcement and guidance for students to consult when speaking with their peers about each assigned daily reading section.

Using Content-Area Graphic Texts for Learning

Lesson demands informing teaching reading with *Smile* and *The Outsiders*

Mr. Merlin's reading-focused language arts lesson plan requires students to be able to read print and non-print texts, interact with different time periods and cultures, and, use reading strategies to help with comprehension. Each of these demands is in the first three IRA/NCTE standards.

Figure 4.2: **What is Mr. Merlin's reading lesson plan asking students to do?** on pages 50–51 addresses four of the twelve IRA/NCTE standards for teaching reading:

- ✦ **Standard 1:** "Students read a wide range of print and non-print texts to build an understanding of texts, of themselves, and of the cultures of the United States and the world; to acquire new information; to respond to the needs and demands of society and the workplace; and for personal fulfillment. Among these texts are fiction and nonfiction, classic and contemporary works."

- ✦ **Standard 2:** "Students read a wide range of literature from many periods in many genres to build an understanding of the many dimensions (e.g., philosophical, ethical, aesthetic) of human experience."

- ✦ **Standard 3:** "Students apply a wide range of strategies to comprehend, interpret, evaluate, and appreciate texts. They draw on their prior experience, their interactions with other readers and writers, their knowledge of word meaning and of other texts, their word identification strategies, and their understanding of textual features (e.g., sound-letter correspondence, sentence structure, context, graphics)."

- ✦ **Standard 10:** "Students whose first language is not English make use of their first language to develop competency in the English language arts and to develop understanding of content across the curriculum."

Aside from these reading standards, students must also rely on basic learning skills to successfully meet these demands. In particular, they must rely on language, higher-order cognition, attention, memory, and sequencing skills for each required step of the assignment.

Language skills are necessary to interpret the "Literate Eye" worksheet, verbally share predictions garnered from each book walk, decode the texts as they read, discuss daily reading assignments, and verbally relate daily reading strategies. They are also essential for following and responding to the others' comments.

Higher-order cognition skills are necessary for any type of analysis. In this lesson, students must understand and apply the directions of the "Literate Eye" handout, analyzing visual and verbal cues as they take the quick book walk and generating discussion comments on the text's elements while reflecting upon others' comments. Students must compare and contrast the different texts and decide how best to relate their impressions to others.

Figure 4.2: What is Mr. Merlin asking his students to do?

Teacher's Instruction	Task Demands On Students	Skills Involved	IRA/NCTE Standards
Hand out two of the "Literate Eye" worksheets; review directions	✦ Read and review the elements of story as they pertain to the "Literate Eye" handout ✦ Focus on Mr. Merlin's explanation of the directions ✦ Keep track of their "Literate Eye" handouts	✦ Attention – focusing on the directions for completing the "Literate Eye" ✦ Language – decoding directions for the "Literate Eye" ✦ Cognition – understanding and applying the directions of the "Literate Eye" handout ✦ Sequencing and memory – identifying the elements of story and recalling and applying them to the "Literate Eye" handouts	**Standard 1** "Students read a wide range of print and non-print texts to build an understanding of texts, of themselves, and of the cultures of the United States and the world; to acquire new information; to respond to the needs and demands of society and the workplace; and for personal fulfillment. Among these texts are fiction and nonfiction, classic and contemporary works." **Standard 3** "Students apply a wide range of strategies to comprehend, interpret, evaluate, and appreciate texts. They draw on their prior experience, their interactions with other readers and writers, their knowledge of word meaning and of other texts, their word identification strategies, and their understanding of textual features (e.g., sound-letter correspondence, sentence structure, context, graphics)."
Divide students into two groups, ask students to perform a book walk through one of two texts and, finally, discuss student predictions based on their book walks	✦ Properly identify the text being assigned to them ✦ Perform a book walk through that text ✦ Discuss predictions garnered from each book walk	✦ Attention – follow the teacher's directions; attend to their proper text assignment ✦ Language – verbally share their predictions based on what they see and read in each text ✦ Cognition – briefly analyze each text as they take a quick book walk ✦ Memory – remember their predictions ✦ Sequencing – state and discuss their predictions in proper order	**Standard 3** "Students apply a wide range of strategies to comprehend, interpret, evaluate, and appreciate texts. They draw on their prior experience, their interactions with other readers and writers, their knowledge of word meaning and of other texts, their word identification strategies, and their understanding of textual features (e.g., sound-letter correspondence, sentence structure, context, graphics)."
Teachers present the directions on the reading schedule	Follow directions for their assigned text's reading schedule	✦ Attention – keep track of what they need to read for each class meeting ✦ Language – decode text as they read ✦ Cognition – read and consider each text's elements of story ✦ Memory – recall each text's elements of story ✦ Sequencing – keep track of where they are in the reading process and be able to recall the elements of story	**Standard 1** "Students read a wide range of print and non-print texts to build an understanding of texts, of themselves, and of the cultures of the United States and the world; to acquire new information; to respond to the needs and demands of society and the workplace; and for personal fulfillment. Among these texts are fiction and nonfiction, classic and contemporary works." **Standard 2** "Students read a wide range of literature from many periods in many genres to build an understanding of the many dimensions (e.g., philosophical, ethical, aesthetic) of human experience."

(continued)

Using Content-Area Graphic Texts for Learning

Teacher's Instruction	Task Demands On Students	Skills Involved	IRA/NCTE Standards
Students will be asked to discuss each day's reading assignment, engage in reading strategies that focus on the elements of story, and update their "Literate Eye" handouts	In pairs, follow each day's directions in their proper order: ✦ Discuss their assigned daily readings ✦ Fill out daily reading strategies focused on the elements of story ✦ Update their "Literate Eye" handouts	✦ Attention – attentively listen to their peers' reading updates ✦ Language – discuss what they have ✦ Cognition – reflect upon and consider each text's elements of story ✦ Memory – recall each text's elements of story and the influence those elements have on the overall stories being told ✦ Sequencing – keep track of each step in these daily directions and fill out their graphic organizers and "Literate Eye" to reflect each day's new sequence of story events	**Standard 1** "Students read a wide range of print and non-print texts to build an understanding of texts, of themselves, and of the cultures of the United States and the world; to acquire new information; to respond to the needs and demands of society and the workplace; and for personal fulfillment. Among these texts are fiction and nonfiction, classic and contemporary works." **Standard 2** "Students read a wide range of literature from many periods in many genres to build an understanding of the many dimensions (e.g., philosophical, ethical, aesthetic) of human experience." **Standard 3** "Students apply a wide range of strategies to comprehend, interpret, evaluate, and appreciate texts. They draw on their prior experience, their interactions with other readers and writers, their knowledge of word meaning and of other texts, their word identification strategies, and their understanding of textual features (e.g., sound-letter correspondence, sentence structure, context, graphics)."

Attention skills are required to focus on all classroom directions, including those given verbally by Mr. Merlin and those written on the "Literate Eye" worksheet. Attention is also necessary to attend to the proper text assignment, monitor their work, ensure they are reading the correct passages and responding to the correct directions, and attend to class and peer group discussions.

Memory skills are necessary as students keep track of Mr. Merlin's directions and to the directions detailed on the "Literate Eye" worksheet. Memory skills are also required, as students must remember their book walk prediction and recall each text's elements of story and the influence those text elements have on the overall stories being told. Finally, when involved in group and class discussions, students must remember what others have said and what they themselves want to contribute, making sure they are not repeating comments made by others.

Sequencing skills are also necessary for students to follow the directions in the correct order, identify story elements and apply them correctly to the "Literate Eye" handouts, state and discuss predictions in the proper order, and keep track of where they are in the reading process. Students must also use sequencing skills to keep track of each step in Mr. Merlin's daily directions, fill out their graphic organizers, and reflect on each day's new sequence of story events. Finally, students must be able to sequence the flow of the various group and classroom discussions.

Teaching writing with middle-level language arts graphic novels

Along with teaching reading with middle-level graphic novels, language arts educators must also teach students about writing middle-level graphic novels. When they add writing to their middle-level language arts lesson plan, teachers can address six more IRA/NCTE standards and, more importantly, encourage creativity and writing skills. The following IRA/NCTE standards, numbered according to their IRA/NCTE indications, are each addressed in the upcoming writing-focused graphic novel lesson plan in middle-level settings (Figure 4.3); note, IRA/NCTE standards ten and eleven are specifically geared toward helping ELLs learn how to write graphic novels as well.

Figure 4.3: IRA/NCTE writing-based standards for teaching middle-level language arts with graphic novels

4. Students adjust their use of spoken, written, and visual language (e.g., conventions, style, vocabulary) to communicate effectively with a variety of audiences and for different purposes.

5. Students employ a wide range of strategies as they write and use different writing process elements appropriately to communicate with different audiences for a variety of purposes.

6. Students apply knowledge of language structure, language conventions (e.g., spelling and punctuation), media techniques, figurative language, and genre to create, critique, and discuss print and non-print texts.

9. Students develop an understanding of and respect for diversity in language use, patterns, and dialects across cultures, ethnic groups, geographic regions, and social roles.

10. Students whose first language is not English make use of their first language to develop competency in the English language arts and to develop understanding of content across the curriculum.

11. Students participate as knowledgeable, reflective, creative, and critical members of a variety of literacy communities.

12. Students use spoken, written, and visual language to accomplish their own purposes (e.g., for learning, enjoyment, persuasion, and the exchange of information).

With these standards in mind, let's once again visit Mr. Merlin's middle-level language arts classroom. During our day-to-day visit, Mr. Merlin moves from a reading-focused lesson plan to a writing-focused lesson plan. Focused on the thought-provoking graphic novel *Americus*

(First Second, 2011) by MK Reed and Jonathan Hill, Mr. Merlin is looking forward to how well his students can build upon their understanding of reading a graphic novel and toward an understanding of writing a graphic novel.

A writing-focused graphic novel lesson plan for middle-level students and their teachers

Goal: Students reflect upon the debate-generating middle-level graphic novel *Americus* (2011), and, in response, write an alternative ending using the key writing components found in graphic novels.

Materials

◆ Copies of the graphic novel *Americus* by MK Reed and Jonathan Hill

◆ Graphic novel formatting handouts, which can be found in a number of sources, such as Bitz's *Manga High* (2011), Monnin's *Teaching Graphic Novels* (2010) or *Teaching Early Reader Comics and Graphic Novels* (2011), Carter's *Building Literacy Connections with Graphic Novels* (2007) or *Super-Powered Word Study* (2010), and online by searching for "graphic novel panel handouts"

◆ Steps handout on pages 57–59

◆ Writing utensils, such as pencils, markers, crayons, colored pencils, and so on

Class Activities

◆ Distribute the steps handout on the following pages to students, and discuss the directions together.

◆ The following NCTE/IRA reading standards apply to the reading part of this lesson plan:

  ◇ **Standard 1:** "Students read a wide range of print and non-print texts to build an understanding of texts, of themselves, and of the cultures of the United States and the world; to acquire new information; to respond to the needs and demands of society and the workplace; and for personal fulfillment. Among these texts are fiction and nonfiction, classic and contemporary works."

  ◇ **Standard 2:** "Students read a wide range of literature from many periods in many genres to build an understanding of the many dimensions (e.g., philosophical, ethical, aesthetic) of human experience."

  ◇ **Standard 3:** "Students apply a wide range of strategies to comprehend, interpret, evaluate, and appreciate texts. They draw on their prior experience, their interactions with other readers and writers, their knowledge of word meaning and of other texts, their word identification strategies, and their understanding of textual features (e.g., sound-letter correspondence, sentence structure, context, graphics)."

- ✦ The following NCTE/IRA standards for teaching writing with middle-level graphic novels apply to the writing part of this lesson plan:
  - ◇ **Standard 4:** "Students adjust their use of spoken, written, and visual language (e.g., conventions, style, vocabulary) to communicate effectively with a variety of audiences and for different purposes."
  - ◇ **Standard 5:** "Students employ a wide range of strategies as they write and use different writing process elements appropriately to communicate with different audiences for a variety of purposes."
  - ◇ **Standard 6:** "Students apply knowledge of language structure, language conventions (e.g., spelling and punctuation), media techniques, figurative language, and genre to create, critique, and discuss print and non-print texts."
  - ◇ **Standard 11:** "Students participate as knowledgeable, reflective, creative, and critical members of a variety of literacy communities."
  - ◇ **Standard 12:** "Students use spoken, written, and visual language to accomplish their own purposes (e.g., for learning, enjoyment, persuasion, and the exchange of information)."

ELL Enrichment

For English language learner enrichment, you may want to make a poster-sized handout of the "Literate Eye." You will also want to choose some key panel elements of story (those focused on plot, setting, characters, themes, rising action, resolution, and climax) and cut them out; ELLs can then paste or tape these key panels in their appropriate places on the poster-sized "Literate Eye." For your teaching convenience, the following is a list of individual panels and page numbers from *Americus* for each of these elements of story.

- ✦ Plot panel examples
  - ◇ pages 82–84 (entire pages or selections), which highlight the main conflict that drives the plot
- ✦ Setting panel examples
  - ◇ page 1 (entire page), the school setting
  - ◇ page 5 (entire page or selections), library setting
  - ◇ page 8 (entire page or selections), the world of Apathea Ravenchilde; pages 88–91 (entire page or selections)
  - ◇ page 11 (entire page or selections), Neil's home
  - ◇ pages 30–31 (entire pages or selections), Danny's home
  - ◇ page 99 (entire page or selections), city hall

Using Content-Area Graphic Texts for Learning

- ✦ Character(s) panel examples
  - ◇ page 12, (entire page) focused on Neil's mom
  - ◇ page 17, (bottom right hand panel), focused on Neil and Danny; page 50 (entire page) focused on Neil and Danny
  - ◇ page 19–20 (entire pages or specific solutions), focused on Neil
  - ◇ pages 30–31 (entire pages or specific selections), focused on Danny's mom
  - ◇ pages 32–34 (entire pages or specific selections), focused on the librarian Charlotte
  - ◇ page 45 (entire page or specific selections), focused on Danny
  - ◇ pages 95 (entire page or specific selections), focused on Neil
- ✦ Theme panel examples
  - ◇ page 17 (final panel, bottom right)
  - ◇ page 29 (middle panel)
  - ◇ page 43 (entire page)
  - ◇ page 49 (last two panels)
  - ◇ page 66
  - ◇ pages 82–83 (all panels)
  - ◇ page 93 (entire page or selections), highlight the theme of freedom of speech and censorship
  - ◇ page 156 (middle row, second panel)
  - ◇ pages 162–163 (all panels)
  - ◇ page 178 (last panel)
  - ◇ page 184 (last panel)
  - ◇ page 189 (last two panels)
  - ◇ page 216
- ✦ Rising action panel examples
  - ◇ page 5 (all panels)
  - ◇ page 30 (final panel)
  - ◇ page 31 (all panels)
  - ◇ page 34 (middle and bottom panels)
  - ◇ page 35 (all panels)
  - ◇ page 45 (final panel)
  - ◇ page 46 (top panel)
  - ◇ page 50 (middle two panels)
  - ◇ page 57 (top panel, far left)
  - ◇ page 66

◇ page 96 (top panel)

◇ page 107 (bottom two panels)

◇ page 159 (top panel)

◇ page 164 (bottom panel)

◇ page 165 (top, second panel)

◇ page 174 (bottom two panels)

◇ page 182 (top and middle panels)

✦ Climax panel examples

◇ page 184 (last panel)

◇ page 186 (all panels)

◇ pages 188–189 (all panels)

✦ Resolution panel examples

◇ page 200, top two panels

◇ page 205, last panel

◇ page 214 (all panels)

◇ page 215 (all panels)

After each element of story panel is copied and cut out, give each ELL individual copies. Next, ask them to select some panels and paste the appropriate panels onto the poster-sized "Literate Eye" handout. In order to further connect the elements of story to reading with graphic novels, teachers should move around the room and conference with ELL students as they make decisions as to where to place their panels (and why).

Teachers will also want to supply their ELLs with ten to fifteen blank panels, which they can use to re-create their own new, alternative ending.

ELL Assessment

✦ Each ELL group will take a turn presenting their rationale and alternative endings to the class.

✦ The NCTE/IRA standards related to teaching ELLs writing with graphic novels are:

◇ **Standard 9:** "Students develop an understanding of and respect for diversity in language use, patterns, and dialects across cultures, ethnic groups, geographic regions, and social roles."

◇ **Standard 10:** "Students whose first language is not English make use of their first language to develop competency in the English language arts and to develop understanding of content across the curriculum."

Handout: Write an Alternative Graphic Novel Ending*

Step 1: Reading Directions

As a class, you will begin by spending three days reading the graphic novel *Americus* by MK Reed and Jonathan Hill. Each day, you will read both in class and at home.

In-class reading

- Day 1: We will start class on the first day by discussing the key terminology you need to know in order to read a graphic novel (teachers, see Appendix). At the end of day 1, you will be offered independent reading time. Ideally, you will be able to read the first three chapters during this time. If you do not finish reading these first three chapters during class, they become homework reading.

- Days 2 and 3: On our second and third class days, we will start with 25–30 minutes of independent reading; during this time each day, you will be expected to read three chapters of *Americus*. What you do not finish in class will become homework reading.

- For the second 25–30 minutes of class on days 2 and 3, you will meet in small groups of 3–4. With your peers, you will be charged with filling out the "Literate Eye" handout.

  At-home reading: Each evening, you will need to finish reading that day's three chapters of assigned reading. Feel free to add to your "Literate Eye" handout while at home as well.

  This daily in-school and out-of-school reading schedule will occur for three days. At the end of these three days, you will have completed your reading of *Americus*, along with your "Literate Eye" handouts.

*See pages 127–131 in the Appendix for a copy-friendly version of this and the "I Write It!" handouts.

Step 2: Writing Directions

For the next three days of our language arts class time, you will meet in small groups. In these groups, you will need to reflect upon the written format of *Americus* and, in doing so, become inspired to draft your own alternative ending to the story. The following steps will help you work through the process of writing an alternative ending.

1. How did the writers of *Americus* end their version of the story? Record your group's thoughts in the panel, gutter, and balloon spaces below.

    ◆ The following **panels** (draw or explain) helped me understand the ending of *Americus*:

    ◆ The following **gutters** (draw or explain) helped me understand the ending of *Americus*:

    ◆ The following **balloons** (draw or explain) helped me understand the ending of *Americus*:

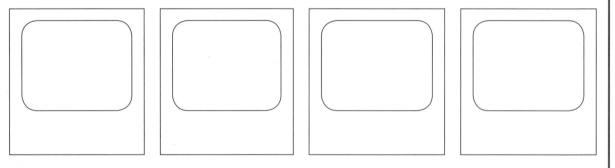

(continued)

2. Think about the three primary audiences for *Americus*: students, parents/family members and, finally, teachers and/or librarians. What do you think each of these audiences will take away from the ending of Reed and Hill's version of *Americus*?

   ✦ Students –

   ✦ Parents/family members –

   ✦ Teachers and/or librarians –

3. If you could rewrite the ending to *Americus*, which audience would you like to write for?

4. Why would you like to write for that audience? What would you want that audience to think about or know at the end of your version of *Americus*?

5. What elements of story, like those found on your "Literate Eye" handouts, would you need to change or alter in order to convince your audience that your ending is the most valid or logical? Use the "I Write It!" handout from your teacher (teachers, see Appendix, modified from *Teaching Graphic Novels*, Monnin, 2010).

6. **Assessment:** Each group will turn in and present their "I Write It!" alternative graphic novel endings. Each group will also need to turn in their "Literate Eye" handouts.

The lesson demands of writing an alternative graphic novel ending

When students write a graphic novel alternative ending, they complement and strengthen their ability to read a graphic novel. As they write their own alternative endings, they vicariously become the literal graphic novel writer—the storyteller responsible for how the panels, gutters, balloons, and their corresponding elements of story can best be expressed in graphic novel format.

Aside from the writing standards that Mr. Merlin's writing lesson addresses (and which are detailed in the section above), students must also rely on basic learning skills to successfully meet these lesson demands. In particular, they must rely on language, higher-order cognition, attention, memory, and sequencing skills for each required step of the assignment.

Language skills are necessary to read and discuss the three-day reading schedule; to read, understand, and note the verbal and visual literacies found in the graphic novel; and to use a rhetorical reading strategy to help connect the visual and verbal aspects of the graphic novel to a visual-based format for telling the story. They are also essential for following and responding to the comments of others. Language skills are called upon when setting up and communicating in groups and are essential when writing alterative endings to *Americus*. Finally, language skills are necessary as students present and relay their group's alternative ending.

Higher-order cognition skills are necessary for any type of creative process, from brainstorming to presentations. In this lesson, students must comprehend the three-day reading schedule directions; distinguish and analyze what verbal and visual literacy components work best together when integrated in a graphic novel; and analyze how what they read in graphic novel format relates and speaks to the elements of story outlined in the "Literate Eye." Finally, higher-order cognitive skills are essential when brainstorming how to create alternative endings in groups, integrate the verbal and visual components on the pages of their graphic novels, and most effectively relay their work to the class.

Attention skills are required for focusing on all classroom directions, including those given verbally by Mr. Merlin and those written on the worksheets. Attention is also essential when working in groups, focusing on what others are saying and how others' comments mesh with their own. Attention is also necessary when attending to the visual and verbal texts and to how the elements of the story can be applied to the "Literate Eye."

Memory skills are necessary to keep track of various written and verbal directions, as well as the three-day reading schedules. Memory skills are also required as students recall the events and elements of story, as well as how and where to place these elements on the "Literate Eye" handout. When interacting with classmates, students must also remember what it is they want to contribute while recalling what the lesson requires of them.

Sequencing skills are necessary for students to follow the directions in the correct order; to identify story elements and apply them correctly to the "Literate Eye" handouts; and to recall the sequential elements of their three-day reading schedule. Sequential processing skills are also essential to work through the directions and logically oragnize their graphic novel alternative endings. Finally, students must rely on sequencing skills when determining how to arrange each of their graphic novel panels in a manner that can be understood by their group members and classmates.

Figure 4.4: Lesson demands emphasized in writing a graphic novel alternative ending, outlines the tasks, skills, and standards addressed in each step of writing an alternative graphic novel ending.

Figure 4.4: Lesson demands emphasized in writing a graphic novel alternative ending

Teacher's Instruction	Task Demands On Students	Skills Involved	IRA/NCTE Standards
Prepare for 3-day reading schedule	Organize into groups; preview and discuss the 3-day reading schedule directions	✦ Attention – identify group members ✦ Language – read and discuss 3-day reading schedule ✦ Cognition – comprehend the 3-day reading schedule directions ✦ Sequencing and memory – remember and plan to follow the 3-day reading schedule	**Reading Standards** 1. "Students read a wide range of print and non-print texts to build an understanding of texts, of themselves, and of the cultures of the United States and the world; to acquire new information; to respond to the needs and demands of society and the workplace; and for personal fulfillment. Among these texts are fiction and nonfiction, classic and contemporary works." 2. "Students read a wide range of literature from many periods in many genres to build an understanding of the many dimensions (e.g., philosophical, ethical, aesthetic) of human experience."
DAY 1 ONLY: Acquaint students with the key terminology involved in reading a graphic novel	Review Appendix and become acquainted with each term and its literary purpose in a graphic novel	✦ Attention – identify group members ✦ Language – read and discuss 3-day reading schedule ✦ Cognition – comprehend the 3-day reading schedule directions ✦ Sequencing and memory – remember and plan to follow the 3-day reading schedule	

(continued)

Teacher's Instruction	Task Demands On Students	Skills Involved	IRA/NCTE Standards
DAYS 1–3: Independent reading	Students read on their own for 25–30 minutes	✦ Attention – focus on reading the graphic novel ✦ Language – read, understand, and note the verbal and visual literacies found in the graphic novel ✦ Cognition – think about how the verbal and visual literacies work together to tell a story in a graphic novel ✦ Sequencing and memory – remember the events and elements of story	3. "Students apply a wide range of strategies to comprehend, interpret, evaluate, and appreciate texts. They draw on their prior experience, their interactions with other readers and writers, their knowledge of word meaning and of other texts, their word identification strategies, and their understanding of textual features (e.g., sound-letter correspondence, sentence structure, context, graphics). 4. "Students adjust their use of spoken, written, and visual language (e.g., conventions, style, vocabulary) to communicate effectively with a variety of audiences and for different purposes."
DAYS 2 and 3 continued: Work in small groups and fill out the "Literate Eye" handout	Students use the "Literate Eye" handout to visually map out all of the major elements of story found in this graphic novel	✦ Attention – given what they have read, students should pay close attention to how the elements of story in the graphic novel can be applied to the "Literate Eye" handout ✦ Language – students use a rhetorical reading strategy to help them connect the visual and verbal aspects of the graphic novel to a visually-based format for telling story ✦ Cognition – think about how what they read in graphic novel format speaks to the elements of story outlined in the "Literate Eye" ✦ Sequencing and memory – remember, and be able to put in proper sequence, each element of story and its proper placement on the "Literate Eye" handout	**Writing Standards** 5. "Students employ a wide range of strategies as they write and use different writing process elements appropriately to communicate with different audiences for a variety of purposes." 6. "Students apply knowledge of language structure, language conventions (e.g., spelling and punctuation), media techniques, figurative language, and genre to create, critique, and discuss print and non-print texts." standing of and respect for diversity in language use, patterns, and dialects across cultures, ethnic groups, geographic regions, and social roles."

(continued)

Teacher's Instruction	Task Demands On Students	Skills Involved	IRA/NCTE Standards
Organize into small groups	Students find group members and organize their initial thoughts about working together	✦ Memory – activate schema about who may be a valuable writing group member ✦ Attention – listen to the directions and follow them accurately ✦ Sequencing – organize into small groups and get ready for the next step ✦ Cognition – prepare to think about work ✦ Language – communicate with peers about potentially working in small groups	9. "Students develop an under10. "Students whose first language is not English make use of their first language to develop competency in the English language arts and to develop understanding of content across the curriculum." 11. "Students participate as knowledgeable, reflective, creative, and critical members of a variety of literacy communities." 12. "Students use spoken, written, and visual language to accomplish their own purposes (e.g., for learning, enjoyment, persuasion, and the exchange of information)."
Read through the directions and, accordingly, write their own alternative graphic novel ending to *Americus*	Students read and work through the directions for writing an alternative graphic novel ending, making use of the graphic novel's unique format (panels, gutters, and balloons)	✦ Memory – recall directions and elements of story from *Americus* ✦ Attention – focus on each individual step in the directions and respond to them accordingly ✦ Sequencing – work through the directions in proper order and also logically organize their graphic novel alternative ending ✦ Cognition – link reading schema to what each direction is asking them to think about ✦ Language – use both verbal and visual literacies to write an alternative ending to *Americus*	
Present alternative graphic novel endings	Memory – recall their group's alternative ending	✦ Attention – concentrate on presenting their own alternative ending and on the presentations of the other groups ✦ Sequencing – be able to present their alternative in a logical, sequential manner ✦ Cognition – think through and discuss both their own graphic novel ending and those of their peers ✦ Language – work with both visual and verbal literacies in order to present their group's alternative ending	

How graphic novels help our five students in language arts

Let's take a brief look at each of our five students and their particular areas of strength and need, especially in terms of reading and writing.

Memory Megan has weak memory skills. Typically in language arts, students like Megan exhibit trouble remembering directions and recalling vocabulary, names, dates, and important story elements and details. Forgetting names, dates, and story details makes it difficult to analyze and discuss.

The graphic novel pairing of visual and verbal information establishes additional memory associations for vocabulary, story elements, and story themes and details. Furthermore, the detailed illustrations help make the material more personal and inviting. The more students can relate to the subject matter, the more memory associations are created. In addition, having Megan pair visual components with her written texts (when creating a graphic novel, for example) not only helps her remember content already read, her visualizing what she *wants* to say and write will help her more effectively communicate as well. Finally, graphic organizers like those provided in the lessons above, help her visualize, link, and recall elements of story with both visual and verbal texts.

Attention Andy is easily distracted and cannot maintain his energy and focus on school-related materials for extended lengths of time. As a result, he exhibits difficulty following stories and attending to plot or character details. Furthermore, he wanders when reading (often missing significant plot turns), and his writing is usually unedited, at times not making sense as he jumps from one topic to the next without sufficiently connecting his ideas. Andy is most successful when presented with short bursts of verbal and visual information, like those found in graphic novel panels and gutters.

Graphic novels provide an excellent means of relaying pertinent information in short visual and verbal bursts. Graphic novels paired with story organizers are even more powerful in helping students like Andy visually and verbally attend to relevant details. Furthermore, the detailed illustrations in graphic novels force students like Andy to slow down as they look and process the multi-sensory details in front of them. The entertaining panels and visual information also make the story content more personal and easier to relate to, which will also invite and encourage longer, sustainable bursts of attention.

Cognitive Coby exhibits weaknesses with higher-order cognition (critically analyzing, problem solving, creating, and brainstorming). This student learner has trouble evaluating, comparing

 *Using Content-Area Graphic Texts for Learning*

and contrasting information, recognizing themes and patterns, creatively expressing new ideas, and interpreting inferences. Each of these skills is essential for critical reading, analytic writing, and creative writing. As a result, teachers who can find ways to break down information into smaller, concrete pieces—like those found in graphic novel panels, gutters, and balloons—help learners like Coby with comprehension.

Graphic novels are helpful for students like Coby as their visual details reinforce the verbal message. The visual/verbal pairing helps make underlying differences, motives, and inferences more obvious and easier to decipher with the multi-sensory data. In addition, the shorter visual/verbal bursts of information relayed are easier to grasp and interpret. Finally, because graphic novel readers must integrate the multi-sensory data, students like Coby get continuous experience integrating and coordinating information. Here, too, the smaller chunks make it easier to integrate the information while providing a lot more experience creating and analyzing data.

Language Larry has difficulty interpreting and understanding what he reads and hears. He also has trouble explaining his ideas when he speaks and writes. This makes language arts a particularly overwhelming challenge for him.

Graphic novels are an excellent language and learning tool for students like Larry as the visual component supports, reinforces, and further develops the verbal message. The concise language of the text and dialogue balloons makes it easier to get the main idea, and the details in the illustrations help students weak in language grasp the more advanced vocabulary, the plot and character details, and the overall social and verbal messages. Furthermore, because there is less language-based text, reading is less overwhelming. Graphic novels empower weak language learners to keep up with the class work and lessons and participate more. As a result, reading and writing become less daunting and more rewarding while effectively meeting and addressing curriculum standards.

Sequence Sue has difficulty remembering and following sequences of text, information, and instruction. This makes following and creating plot sequences and stories particularly challenging. While language art students like Sue can likely remember and comprehend what is read, they exhibit trouble recalling and putting those details in order.

Graphic novels are excellent learning tools for students with sequential processing weaknesses. Reading graphic novels is all about following and integrating small verbal and visual story chunks. Graphic organizes further aid in recalling series of events. Furthermore, there is added value with using graphic novels as the verbal and visual cues complement each other and reinforce the sequence of events.

Conclusion and suggested graphic novels for middle-level language arts instruction

Mr. Merlin feels pretty lucky to be a language arts teacher. "Why?" we may wonder. "It is to us, my satisfied language arts teachers, that graphic novels belong," he might say.

Fortunate and grateful, language arts teachers stand at the top of the totem pole of teaching content-area graphic novels. For it is the language arts teachers who have the best vantage point from which to utilize not only a valuable, modern literacy learning text, but also an extremely popular middle-level text.

Figure 4.5, on pages 67–72, presents a thematic list of suggested middle-level language arts graphic novels. And because there are so many opportunities to match language arts instruction with middle-level graphic novels, we encourage you to post your new finds and suggestions on our blog site at http://departingthetext.blogspot.com.

Figure 4.5: Thematic list of middle-level language arts graphic novels

Title and Author	Act of Reading	Action-Adventure	Bravery	Coming of Age	Community	Culture	Diversity and Caring	Domestic Relations	Fairy Tales, Fables, and Folklore	Family	Fate, Destiny, and/or Chance	Foreign Relations	Friendship	Gender	Good and Evil	Heroes and Villains	Historical Context	Humanitarianism	Humor	Identity	Leadership	Loyalty and Trust	Myth and Legend	Narration	Plot Twists and Turns	Point of View	Relationships	School Life	Science Fiction	Space	Tradition	World Travel
Adventures in Cartooning: How to Turn Your Doodles Into Comics by James Sturm, Andrew Arnold, and Alexis Frederick-Frost	X	X	X						X							X			X				X	X	X							
Amelia Rules! Superheroes by Jimmy Gownley		X	X	X									X	X		X			X	X							X	X				
Americus by MK Reed and Jonathan Hill	X	X	X	X	X	X	X	X		X		X	X	X	X						X					X	X	X				
Amulet by Kazu Kibuishi*		X	X	X						X	X		X	X	X	X			X	X	X				X		X		X			
Anya's Ghost by Vera Brosgol			X	X			X			X	X		X	X	X				X	X							X	X				
The Baby-Sitters Club: Kristy's Great Idea by Raina Telgemeier*				X									X	X					X	X							X	X				
Bake Sale by Sara Varon							X						X						X	X							X					
Beowulf by Gareth Hinds									X		X				X						X	X	X									
Bone by Jeff Smith*		X	X	X	X				X		X	X			X	X			X	X	X	X	X		X		X					
Boys Only: How to Survive Anything by Martin Oliver and Simon Ecob		X	X												X						X											
Brain Camp by Susan Kim, Laurence Klavan, and Faith Erin Hicks	X	X		X	X		X						X	X					X	X						X	X	X				
Buddha by Osamu Tezuka*		X	X	X	X						X				X	X	X	X	X	X	X		X		X		X					
Buzzboy: Sidekicks Rule! by John Gallagher		X	X	X											X	X			X	X	X				X		X	X				

Theme

Theme

Title and Author	Act of Reading	Action-Adventure	Bravery	Coming of Age	Community	Culture	Diversity and Caring	Domestic Relations	Fairy Tales, Fables, and Folklore	Family	Fate, Destiny, and/or Chance	Foreign Relations	Friendship	Gender	Good and Evil	Heroes and Villains	Historical Context	Humanitarianism	Humor	Identity	Leadership	Loyalty and Trust	Myth and Legend	Narration	Plot Twists and Turns	Point of View	Relationships	School Life	Science Fiction	Space	Tradition	World Travel
Cardboard by Doug TenNapel	X	X	X	X	X					X			X		X												X		X			
Cat Burglar Black by Richard Sala		X	X	X	X					X			X	X	X						X				X		X	X				
Creature Tech by Doug TenNapel		X	X	X	X			X		X		X			X					X					X		X		X			
The Cryptics by Steve Niles and Ben Roman	X	X			X		X						X		X	X			X	X					X		X		X			
The Dark Knight Returns by Frank Miller, Klaus Janson, and Lynn Varley		X	X	X	X			X			X					X		X	X						X							
Dawn Land by Joseph Bruchac, and Will Davis			X	X	X	X	X	X		X				X				X		X	X	X	X									
The Demon of River Heights (Nancy Drew, Girl Detective #1) by Stefan Petrucha and Sho Murase*		X		X							X		X	X	X	X					X	X			X						X	
Female Force by Neal Bailey	X			X	X	X	X	X		X				X			X	X		X	X											
Feynman by Jim Ottaviani and Leland Myrick		X	X	X	X	X	X	X						X			X	X	X	X							X		X			
Flight: Volume One, edited by Kazu Kibuishi	X	X		X					X	X	X		X	X	X	X			X	X		X	X	X			X	X	X	X	X	X
Foiled by Jane Yolen and Mike Cavallaro*		X	X	X			X			X			X	X				X						X	X		X				X	
Forget Sorrow: An Ancestral Tale by Belle Yang		X	X	X		X	X			X			X	X	X		X			X		X	X	X	X		X					X
G-Man by Chris Giarrusso*	X	X	X	X						X			X		X	X			X	X			X		X		X	X				

(continued)

Theme

Title and Author	Act of Reading	Action-Adventure	Bravery	Coming of Age	Community	Culture	Diversity and Caring	Domestic Relations	Fairy Tales, Fables, and Folklore	Family	Fate, Destiny, and/or Chance	Foreign Relations	Friendship	Gender	Good and Evil	Heroes and Villains	Historical Context	Humanitarianism	Humor	Identity	Leadership	Loyalty and Trust	Myth and Legend	Narration	Plot Twists and Turns	Point of View	Relationships	School Life	Science Fiction	Space	Tradition	World Travel
Girls Only: How to Survive Anything by Martin Oliver and Daniela Geremia		X	X												X						X											
Give It Up! And Other Short Stories by Franz Kafka and Peter Kuper		X	X	X	X		X	X		X	X				X		X	X	X						X		X					
Hatter M: The Looking Glass Wars by Frank Beddor, Liz Cavalier, and Ben Templesmith		X	X	X	X	X	X	X	X	X	X	X		X	X		X	X	X	X		X			X		X					
Hereville: How Mirka Got Her Sword by Barry Deutsch		X	X	X	X		X		X	X				X	X						X		X								X	
The Homeland Directive by Robert Venditti and Mike Huddleston		X	X	X		X		X				X	X	X	X		X	X			X	X			X							
Identity Crisis by Brad Meltzer		X	X	X	X	X	X				X		X	X	X	X		X		X	X								X			
The Invention of Hugo Cabret by Brian Selznick	X	X	X								X																					
Journey into Mohawk Country by George O'Connor	X	X		X	X	X	X	X				X	X				X			X		X		X	X		X					X
The Jungle Book adapted by Dan Johnson and Amit Tayal		X		X									X		X		X		X	X	X						X					
Kaput and Zösky by Lewis Trondheim and Eric Cartier*		X						X		X	X	X				X		X	X	X	X				X		X		X	X		
Kid Beowulf by Alexis Fajado		X	X	X						X	X	X				X	X	X	X	X	X		X				X	X			X	
King Lear adapted by Gareth Hinds					X			X		X		X		X		X				X						X						

(continued)

Title and Author	Act of Reading	Action-Adventure	Bravery	Coming of Age	Community	Culture	Diversity and Caring	Domestic Relations	Fairy Tales, Fables, and Folklore	Family	Fate, Destiny, and/or Chance	Foreign Relations	Friendship	Gender	Good and Evil	Heroes and Villains	Historical Context	Humanitarianism	Humor	Identity	Leadership	Loyalty and Trust	Myth and Legend	Narration	Plot Twists and Turns	Point of View	Relationships	School Life	Science Fiction	Space	Tradition	World Travel
Knights of the Lunch Table: The Dodgeball Chronicles by Frank Cammuso*	X	X	X	X	X								X						X	X	X				X			X				
Koko Be Good by Jen Wang				X	X	X	X						X	X	X				X	X				X		X	X					
The Last Dragon by Jane Yolen and Rebecca Guay			X	X					X		X		X	X	X	X			X				X		X							
Lex Luthor: Man of Steel by Brian Azzarello and Lee Bermejo		X	X					X			X					X	X								X							
Locklaw and the Pet Avengers by Chris Eliopoulos and Ig Guara*		X	X	X	X								X			X			X	X	X							X				
The Complete Maus by Art Spiegelman	X		X	X	X	X	X	X		X	X	X	X		X	X	X		X	X				X		X	X					
The Merchant of Venice adapted by Gareth Hinds					X								X	X					X	X		X					X					
Middle School is Worse Than Meatloaf: A Year Told Through Stuff by Jennifer L. Holm and Elicia Castaldi	X			X						X			X							X								X				
The Mighty Skullboy Army by Jacob Chabot	X	X	X	X	X		X	X		X	X	X	X		X	X					X				X	X	X	X	X			
No Fear Shakespeare* by SparkNotes		X	X	X										X						X	X				X	X					X	X
The Odyssey adapted by Gareth Hinds		X	X	X	X			X		X	X	X			X				X		X	X										

(continued)

Theme

Title and Author	Act of Reading	Action-Adventure	Bravery	Coming of Age	Community	Culture	Diversity and Caring	Domestic Relations	Fairy Tales, Fables, and Folklore	Family	Fate, Destiny, and/or Chance	Foreign Relations	Friendship	Gender	Good and Evil	Heroes and Villains	Historical Context	Humanitarianism	Humor	Identity	Leadership	Loyalty and Trust	Myth and Legend	Narration	Plot Twists and Turns	Point of View	Relationships	School Life	Science Fiction	Space	Tradition	World Travel
Oliver Twist, adapted by Dan Johnson and Rajesh Nagulakonda				X	X	X				X	X	X					X			X		X			X							
Orcs: Forged for War by Stan Nicholls and Joe Flood		X	X	X	X	X	X	X	X			X		X	X					X	X	X	X		X		X					
Page by Paige by Laura Lee Gulledge	X			X	X	X				X			X	X						X				X		X	X					
The Picture of Dorian Gray adapted by Roy Thomas and Sebastian Fiumara				X					X		X									X												
Photo Booth by Lewis Helfand and Sachin Nagar			X					X		X	X						X			X	X	X			X		X					
Resistance: Book 1 by Carla Jablonski and Leland Purvis*		X	X	X	X	X	X	X		X	X	X	X	X			X	X		X	X						X					
Sherlock Holmes, Vol. 1 by Leah Moore, John Reppion, and Aaron Campbell												X	X							X					X	X						
Sita: Daughter of the Earth by Saraswati Nagpal		X	X	X	X	X	X	X		X		X		X	X		X	X		X	X		X			X	X				X	X
Skullkickers by Jim Zub, Edwin Huang, and Misty Coats		X	X												X	X					X								X			
Smile by Raina Telgemeier	X			X	X	X	X	X		X			X	X			X		X	X				X			X	X				
Space Race by CEL Welsh and K.L. Jones					X	X	X			X							X	X		X						X	X		X			X

(continued)

71

Theme

Title and Author	Act of Reading	Action-Adventure	Bravery	Coming of Age	Community	Culture	Diversity and Caring	Domestic Relations	Fairy Tales, Fables, and Folklore	Family	Fate, Destiny, and/or Chance	Foreign Relations	Friendship	Gender	Good and Evil	Heroes and Villains	Historical Context	Humanitarianism	Humor	Identity	Leadership	Loyalty and Trust	Myth and Legend	Narration	Plot Twists and Turns	Point of View	Relationships	School Life	Science Fiction	Space	Tradition	World Travel
Star Wars: Clone Wars Adventures, Vol. 1 by Haden Blackman, Matt Fillbach, Shawn Fillbach, and Ben Caldwell*		×	×	×			×			×	×	×	×		×			×		×	×	×	×		×	×			×	×		
Superman: Birthright by Mark Waid, Leinil Francis Yu, and Gerry Alanguilan		×	×	×							×				×	×		×		×	×			×			×	×	×	×		
Superman: Red Son by Mark Millar, David Johnson, Kilian Plunkett, Andrew Robinson, and Walden Wong		×	×	×	×	×	×	×			×	×			×	×							×		×	×			×	×	×	
Tribes by Michael Geszel, Peter Spinetta, Inaki Miranda, and Eva De La Cruz*		×	×	×	×	×	×			×	×	×	×	×	×			×				×	×				×					
Trickster: Native American Tales: A Graphic Collection, edited by Matt Dembicki			×	×	×	×	×	×	×	×	×	×					×															
Whatever Happened to the World of Tomorrow? by Brian Fies		×		×		×		×		×		×			×		×				×					×			×			
Zahra's Paradise by Amir and Khalil	×		×	×	×	×	×	×		×	×	×					×	×	×	×	×	×			×	×	×				×	×
Zita the Spacegirl by Ben Hatke		×	×	×					×			×	×						×	×	×						×	×				

72

Graphic Novels in the Social Studies Classroom

Graphic novels lend themselves to content-area social studies. Whether they depict "mild-mannered" characters or metal-bending, train-stopping superheroes in stories of fiction, nonfiction, historical fiction, fantasy, or science fiction, graphic novels are all about communities, developing identities, social organizations, rites of passage, and forms of governance.

Aside from their story content, graphic novels engage readers as they construct and integrate the verbal and visual components of story. This makes content easier to grasp and recall. But most importantly, graphic novels provide outstanding springboards for learning and class discussions as they *make* the content come alive.

To help you integrate graphic novels into your social studies classrooms, this chapter presents:

1. An overview of how graphic novels can help different student learners tackle social studies material;

2. A specific, graphic novel-based social studies lesson plan;

3. A discussion of what the graphic novel social studies lesson is asking students to do—focusing on curriculum standards and five learning skills (attention, memory, language, sequencing, and cognition);

4. An alignment to the appropriate social studies Common Core Standards;

5. An illuminating discussion on how graphic novels will help five familiar yet different types of learners succeed in your social studies classrooms; and

6. A lengthy bibliography of suggested graphic novels for social studies classrooms.

How graphic novels help students in social studies: a general overview

Children's graphic novels are rife with social studies content. Many graphic novels relate nonfiction or fictional retellings of historical events or are set in future or parallel worlds. All graphic novels deal with people, places, and environments and revolve around themes of personal and/or cultural growth. Most graphic novels also deal with issues of power, authority and governance, and individuals or institutions, and many deal with civic ideas and practices. Many also revolve around science and technology and their growing influence on individuals and society. Each of these topics has been designated by the National Council for the Social Studies and the Common Core Standards.

Graphic novels can and should be used to illustrate and reinforce these Common Core curricular themes. They make the subject matter more personal and allow readers to construct working theories of social, political, economic, historical, anthropological, and geographic models. Graphic novels naturally integrate Common Core Standards in an interactive, multi-sensory manner. The art and visual images in these volumes help make the material more personal as they invite the reader to participate in the story. Students have to integrate the verbal and visual messages while filling in the gutters' gaps and constructing the complete story. This makes reading these books a very active, personal experience. Furthermore, the visual components complement and reinforce the verbal message, and students find the format inviting and motivating.

With these overall benefits in mind, we now take a closer look at how graphic novels can be integrated into social studies classrooms. Our teacher, Mr. Schindler, is teaching his fifth-grade unit on World War II. While no relation to the famous Schindler, he uses his name to his advantage during this unit.

Mr. Schindler is about to travel with his students to France as Germany begins its occupation in 1940. Before discussing military strategies, famous battles, and speeches, Mr. Schindler wants his students to better understand what life was like for French citizens in 1940. He believes the more his students can relate to that time period, the more they will understand and retain.

The lesson he shares below has two parts and can be conducted over two or more periods (depending on how many of our additional options you choose to include). The first part takes a look at a specific event in modern world history (the German invasion of France in World War II) from the perspective of three children in Carla Jablonski and Leland Purvis' *Resistance* (First Second Books, 2010). The second part of the lesson integrates this story with a German

propaganda newsreel from that time period. It asks students to infer how the children in *Resistance* might have reacted to the propaganda while evaluating the role propaganda plays.

This lesson neatly addresses Common Core social studies *and* reading curriculum standards. In brief, this lessons incorporates social studies standards addressing culture and cultural diversity; people, places, and historical events; individual development and identity; issues of power, authority, and governance; global connections; and civic ideals and practices. It also incorporates Common Core reading standards addressing key ideas and details, craft and structure, and the integration of knowledge and ideas. However, this lesson goes even further as it addresses visual literacy while examining the juxtaposition of image and text to influence others.

Following the lesson's presentation, we will delineate the Common Core Standards the lesson addresses and the learning demands it places on your students. The remainder of the chapter will discuss how the lesson addresses the learning needs of our five students, followed by a suggested reading list for your and your students.

A social studies lesson using graphic novels

Goal: To recognize and understand the ramifications of a divided (occupied vs. free) France at the onset of World War II and the power of propaganda.

Materials

- ✦ *Resistance* by Carla Jablonski and Leland Purvis (First Second Books, 2010)
- ✦ Film footage of the German invasion of France, along with broadcasts of the French surrender and of Franco/German propaganda: www.youtu.be/13zes7ASkdU
- ✦ Optional map resources
    - ◇ www.worldwar2database.com/html/france.htm
    - ◇ An engaging, animated map detailing the fall of France: www.bbc.co.uk/history/worldwars/wwtwo/launch_ani_fall_france_campaign.shtml
- ✦ Optional reading resources
    - ◇ Vichy France, 1940–1944: www.warhistory.ie/world-war-2/battle-of-france.htm
    - ◇ World War II and the fall of France: www.bbc.co.uk/history/worldwars/wwtwo/fall_france_01.shtml
    - ◇ The French Resistance: www.historylearningsite.co.uk/french_resistance.htm
    - ◇ An interactive virtual tour of World War II artifacts, documents, photos, and weapons: www.museumofworldwarii.com/TourText/Area05_Intelligence.htm

◇ Visual clips of archived French and German World War II photographs: www.youtu.be/nnCvshnHrco

Class Activities

Part I: The ramifications of a divided France at the onset of World War II

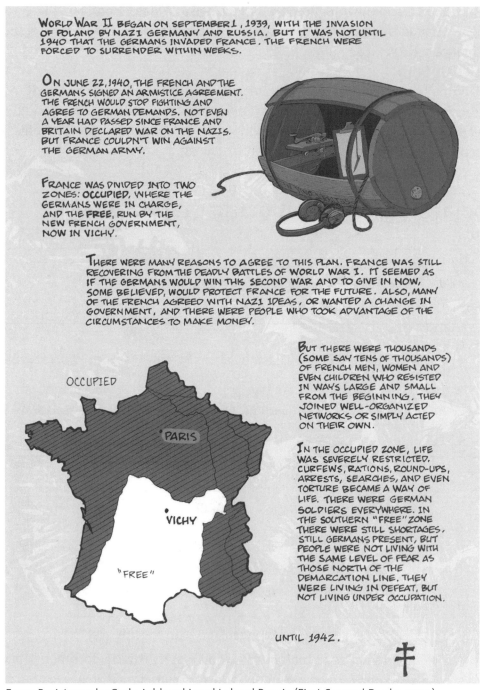

WORLD WAR II BEGAN ON SEPTEMBER 1, 1939, WITH THE INVASION OF POLAND BY NAZI GERMANY AND RUSSIA. BUT IT WAS NOT UNTIL 1940 THAT THE GERMANS INVADED FRANCE. THE FRENCH WERE FORCED TO SURRENDER WITHIN WEEKS.

ON JUNE 22, 1940, THE FRENCH AND THE GERMANS SIGNED AN ARMISTICE AGREEMENT. THE FRENCH WOULD STOP FIGHTING AND AGREE TO GERMAN DEMANDS. NOT EVEN A YEAR HAD PASSED SINCE FRANCE AND BRITAIN DECLARED WAR ON THE NAZIS. BUT FRANCE COULDN'T WIN AGAINST THE GERMAN ARMY.

FRANCE WAS DIVIDED INTO TWO ZONES: OCCUPIED, WHERE THE GERMANS WERE IN CHARGE, AND THE FREE, RUN BY THE NEW FRENCH GOVERNMENT, NOW IN VICHY.

THERE WERE MANY REASONS TO AGREE TO THIS PLAN. FRANCE WAS STILL RECOVERING FROM THE DEADLY BATTLES OF WORLD WAR I. IT SEEMED AS IF THE GERMANS WOULD WIN THIS SECOND WAR AND TO GIVE IN NOW, SOME BELIEVED, WOULD PROTECT FRANCE FOR THE FUTURE. ALSO, MANY OF THE FRENCH AGREED WITH NAZI IDEAS, OR WANTED A CHANGE IN GOVERNMENT, AND THERE WERE PEOPLE WHO TOOK ADVANTAGE OF THE CIRCUMSTANCES TO MAKE MONEY.

BUT THERE WERE THOUSANDS (SOME SAY TENS OF THOUSANDS) OF FRENCH MEN, WOMEN AND EVEN CHILDREN WHO RESISTED IN WAYS LARGE AND SMALL FROM THE BEGINNING. THEY JOINED WELL-ORGANIZED NETWORKS OR SIMPLY ACTED ON THEIR OWN.

IN THE OCCUPIED ZONE, LIFE WAS SEVERELY RESTRICTED. CURFEWS, RATIONS, ROUND-UPS, ARRESTS, SEARCHES, AND EVEN TORTURE BECAME A WAY OF LIFE. THERE WERE GERMAN SOLDIERS EVERYWHERE. IN THE SOUTHERN "FREE" ZONE THERE WERE STILL SHORTAGES, STILL GERMANS PRESENT, BUT PEOPLE WERE NOT LIVING WITH THE SAME LEVEL OF FEAR AS THOSE NORTH OF THE DEMARCATION LINE. THEY WERE LIVING IN DEFEAT, BUT NOT LIVING UNDER OCCUPATION.

OCCUPIED

PARIS

VICHY

"FREE"

UNTIL 1942.

From *Resistance* by Carla Jablonski and Leland Purvis (First Second Books, 2010)

Using Content-Area Graphic Texts for Learning

- Introduce and present background facts and events leading to Germany's occupation of a divided France.

- Have students read the first-page introduction of *Resistance: Book 1*, which briefly describes the onset of World War II and the German occupation of France.

- Optional: Divide the class into three to five groups. Have each group evaluate one of the optional resources above and make a two-minute class presentation relaying the information from that resource. Make sure their presentations address how they think these events affected French children their age at that time. For example: fathers and teachers going to war, shortages of food, fear, roundups of Jewish people, and men forced to serve and "rebuild."

- Discussion:
    ◇ How do you think the French felt as Nazi troops marched into Paris?
    ◇ How do you think life was different in *occupied* France versus *free* France? Where would you prefer to be? Why?

- Have students read *Resistance: Book 1*. This is a story of life in France as it follows two French families: the Levys (Jewish) and the Tessiers (not Jewish). The story depicts life decisions *each* family member must make to (a) support the Nazis, (b) survive with no involvement, or (c) join the French Resistance.

- Break the class into five groups, each one representing one of the book's characters: Paul Tessier, Henri Levy, Jacques, Mrs. Tessier, and Marie Tessier.

- Have each group prepare a news interview or

From *Resistance* by Carla Jablonski and Leland Purvis (First Second Books, 2010)

Chapter 5: Graphic Novels in the Social Studies Classroom

a life-event re-enactment for each of their characters. The news interview or re-enactment must relay:

◇ How they felt and reacted when they heard France was occupied

◇ The obstacles and problems they are currently faced with

◇ How they plan to address their problems

◇ What they think their situation will be in one year's time.

✦ Have each group present their interview or reenactment.

✦ Optional: Discuss class reactions to these interviews/reenactments.

Part II: The role propaganda can play

✦ While watching this video clip, www.youtu.be/13zes7ASkdU, have students fill in the middle two columns of the worksheet (Figure 5.1). Instruct students to fill in the middle two columns of the worksheet ("List the key words used in the message" and "Describe the images used with the message") as they watch the clip.

◇ Note that while this worksheet incorporates the video clip, students can also work on columns one, two, and four (ignoring having to describe the images of the message) if you chose not to use the video clip, as we have provided the verbal content of the German propaganda segments.

✦ Review how students filled in the two middle columns.

✦ Break students into three groups—one for each news item found on the worksheet. Have student groups respond to the third column of the worksheet ("For discussion"), which evaluates and compares the content of the ACE news film with that of *Resistance: Book 1*.

✦ Have students present their group's responses to the class.

✦ Conclude with a discussion on the use and function of propaganda and its effectiveness.

◇ Compare the German-controlled "news" messages and the visual images relayed.

◇ Note that in WWII, there was no television, Internet, or YouTube. Film clips were only available in the movies. Most people heard news on the radio or read it in newspapers. How does the addition of the visual image affect the message?

◇ How effective do you think this propaganda would have been for Jacques or the Tessier family?

◇ Discuss how propaganda was relayed then and how it is relayed today. What is the same? What is different?

◇ Optional: Discuss *how* to evaluate news reports.

Using Content-Area Graphic Texts for Learning

Figure 5.1: World War II French occupation and propaganda worksheet

News item	List the key words used in the message	Describe the images used with the message	For discussion
"The retreating British army set fire to Lorient's oil tanks … thus harming their former allies … It was only thanks to German firemen … that the blaze was extinguished and the fuel saved."			Discussion: Who would benefit most from saving the fuel? Why? How do you think Jacques (from *Resistance: Book 1)* and the Resistance might interpret this news item?
"In the occupied zone, the Germans are mustering … every able-bodied man to erase all traces of war … Most of the French rail network … is in service again."			Discussion: What were the benefits of the Germans having the French "erase all traces" of the war? How might have the destruction and the rebuilding of Paris affected Sophie, Marie, Paul, and Henri's "mission?" How might it have affected other members of the Resistance in Paris?
"The ladies of the German Red Cross help everywhere … German aid organizations … bring relief to refugees returning to their homes in the occupied zone … food distributions in Montmartre."			Discussion: Describe the faces of the children in this segment of the film clip. Is this food distribution helping them? Why/why not? How is the information in the photo different from the text? In *Resistance*, pages 21–23, Paul's aunt describes the situation in Paris: "They rounded up hundreds—thousands. Mostly women and children. You could hear the crying, the screaming. They kept them there in the Vélodrome d'Hiver for days. No food, no water … My beautiful Paris has changed dreadfully." How does the film's depiction of France compare to Paul's aunt's description?

*See page 132 in the Appendix for a copy-friendly version of this handout.

The lesson's demands

As indicated in Figure 5.2 ("What is this lesson asking students to do?", pages 82–85), this lesson addresses multiple Common Core Standards that, in turn, demand multiple learning skills. This lesson requires students to process and understand the following core standards in social studies:

+ Culture and Cultural Diversity – students evaluate the French reaction to German invasion and how life changed for the French with the invasion as they analyze the news releases and the use of propaganda;

+ Time, Continuity, and Change – students analyze and understand past historical events and concepts of propaganda, occupation, resistance, and surrender, to name a few;

+ People, Places, and Environments – students relate their personal experiences to happenings in France under German occupation in WWII;

+ Individual Development and Identity – students examine how the graphic novel's characters reacted to major life changes and developed their sense of self;

+ Individuals, Groups, and Institutions – students examine the ways in which French and German institutions addressed human needs, change over time, social conformity, and influence of cultures;

+ Power, Authority, and Governance – students evaluate the rights and responsibilities of the various French and German citizens and leaders;

+ Production, Distribution, and Consumption – students evaluate the role of technology (war machines, news media, transportation options) in France during WWII and how these technologies affected and transformed the lives of individuals and institutions;

+ Global Connections – students examine the interactions of French citizens, the French Resistance, occupied vs. free France, and the occupying Germans; and

+ Civic Ideals and Practices – students evaluate the roles individual citizens such as Jacques, the Tessiers, and the Levys played in their communities.

Aside from these social studies standards, students must also process multiple Common Core language arts standards as they read, write, and communicate their thoughts and findings. We include these standards in the following table. To successfully meet these demands, students must rely on verbal and visual language processing, higher-order cognition, attention, memory, and the sequencing of information within each required step of the assignment.

Language skills are necessary to read and follow Mr. Schindler's directions, read required texts, and participate in class discussions and worksheets. Students must also use language skills when evaluating the ACE newscast and when writing their character interviews or visual reenactments.

Higher-order cognition skills are necessary for analyzing, brainstorming, creating, and evaluating information. In this lesson, they are employed to understand the worksheet and Mr. Schindler's directions, evaluate what life was like for children in France during WWII, create and answer character interviews/reenactments for students' selected *Resistance* character, evaluate the ACE newscast, and recognize and analyze propaganda materials. Higher-order cognition skills are also necessary to follow, analyze, and contribute thoughtful content to the closing discussion.

Attention skills are necessary for students to focus on Mr. Schindler's directions, discussions, and watching the ACE newscast. Attention is also necessary to read the map on page 1 of *Resistance*. Students also have to focus on filling in the correct portions of the worksheet and monitor their progress as they work through the class lesson.

Memory skills are necessary for students to remember Mr. Schindler's directions, the story details in *Resistance*, and the ACE newscast details. They have to recall these details for class discussions, when creating their character interviews, and when working on their worksheets (Figure 5.2).

Sequencing skills are necessary for students to follow the directions in the correct order. Students also have to complete the worksheet in the correct order, filling in the middle columns while watching the ACE newscast and filling in the column to the right after reading *Resistance* and watching the newscast. Students must also follow the flow of Mr. Schindler's introduction, the course of Hitler's invasion of France, the storyline in *Resistance*, and the course and sequence of the class discussions.

Figure 5.2: What is this lesson asking students to do?

Teacher's Instruction	Task Demands On Students	Skills Involved	Common Core Standards*
Read the first-page introduction of *Resistance: Book 1*, and discuss how the French felt and how life was different in occupied France versus free France.	◆ Focus on the directions ◆ Read the introduction and analyze its map ◆ Brainstorm how the French felt and how life was different for occupied vs. free France	◆ Attention – to directions, the map and text, and the class discussion ◆ Language – decoding text and expressing opinions ◆ Memory – recalling instructions and information from the introduction ◆ Cognition – analyzing the introduction and brainstorming what life in France must have been like ◆ Sequencing – remembering teacher instructions and the flow of discussions	◆ Culture and Cultural Diversity (NCSS) ◆ People, Places, and Environments (NCSS) ◆ Individuals, Groups, and Institutions (NCSS) ◆ Power, Authority, and Governance (NCSS) ◆ Production, Distribution, and Consumption (NCSS) ◆ Global Connections (NCSS) ◆ Integration of Knowledge and Ideas (R/LA) ◆ Craft and Structure (R/LA) ◆ Key Ideas and Details (R/LA) ◆ Compare and Contrast Content (R/LA) ◆ Range of Reading and Level of Text Complexity (R/LA)
Read *Resistance: Book 1*.	◆ Read text while attending to illustrations ◆ Construct a better understanding of occupied and free France and how the Tessier and Levy families address their challenges	◆ Attention – to flow of panels, the text, and the details in the artwork ◆ Language – decoding and interpreting text; picking up social and emotional nuances ◆ Memory – keeping the historical details from the introduction in mind as they follow and remember the story line ◆ Cognition – recognizing and interpreting verbal and visual nuances as they gain greater insight into the story and its characters ◆ Sequencing – following the flow and sequence of panels and text; keeping track of the story	◆ Culture and Cultural Diversity (NCSS) ◆ Time, Continuity, and Change (NCSS) ◆ People, Places, and Environments (NCSS) ◆ Individual Development and Identity (NCSS) ◆ Individuals, Groups, and Institutions (NCSS) ◆ Power, Authority, and Governance (NCSS) ◆ Production, Distribution, and Consumption (NCSS) ◆ Global Connections (NCSS) ◆ Civic Ideals and Practices (NCSS) ◆ Integration of Knowledge and Ideas (R/LA) ◆ Craft and Structure (R/LA) ◆ Key Ideas and Details (R/LA) ◆ Compare and Contrast Content (R/LA) ◆ Range of Reading and Level of Text Complexity (R/LA)

(continued)

Teacher's Instruction	Task Demands On Students	Skills Involved	Common Core Standards*
Each group prepares a news interview or a life-event re-enactment for each of their characters.	◆ Recall each point they must cover ◆ Create a profile for their character, reflecting how he/she felt/reacted to Germany's invasion, the obstacles he/she faced, and how he/she planned to meet those obstacles ◆ Present the profile to the class	◆ Attention – attending to story details in order to prepare a thorough interview; making sure all three discussion points are addressed ◆ Language – following the directions; making sure to ask and answer the right questions for the interview ◆ Memory – remembering the story well enough to create an interview; remembering what the lesson demands are ◆ Cognition – understanding the story and characters of Resistance; creating interview questions and responses that address the lesson's demands ◆ Sequencing – following the lesson's directions; making sure the interview questions flow and makes sense	◆ Culture and Cultural Diversity (NCSS) ◆ Time, Continuity, and Change (NCSS) ◆ People, Places, and Environments (NCSS) ◆ Individual Development and Identity (NCSS) ◆ Individuals, Groups, and Institutions (NCSS) ◆ Power, Authority, and Governance (NCSS) ◆ Production, Distribution, and Consumption (NCSS) ◆ Global Connections (NCSS) ◆ Civic Ideals and Practices (NCSS) ◆ Integration of Knowledge and Ideas (R/LA) ◆ Craft and Structure (R/LA) ◆ Key Ideas and Details (R/LA) ◆ Compare and Contrast Content (R/LA)
Review the worksheet and introduce the video clip to students.	◆ Focus on directions ◆ Recognize how to fill in the rows and columns appropriately ◆ Keep directions in mind as the film is watched and the worksheet is filled in	◆ Attention – to follow the directions ◆ Language – understanding the directions and what is required; understanding verbal data relayed on the video and worksheet ◆ Memory – remembering the directions ◆ Cognition – understanding and evaluating the intent of the video and Mr. Mengel's direction ◆ Sequencing – following the directions in the correct sequence and filling in the correct boxes	◆ Culture and Cultural Diversity (NCSS) ◆ Time, Continuity, and Change (NCSS) ◆ People, Places, and Environments (NCSS) ◆ Individual Development and Identity (NCSS) ◆ Individuals, Groups, and Institutions (NCSS) ◆ Power, Authority, and Governance (NCSS) ◆ Production, Distribution, and Consumption (NCSS) ◆ Global Connections (NCSS) ◆ Civic Ideals and Practices (NCSS) ◆ Integration of Knowledge and Ideas (R/LA) ◆ Craft and Structure (R/LA) ◆ Key Ideas and Details (R/LA) ◆ Compare and Contrast Content (R/LA)

(continued)

Teacher's Instruction	Task Demands On Students	Skills Involved	Common Core Standards*
Students watch the video clip, filling in the two middle columns as it is being watched.	◆ Decode text and images while filling in the worksheet ◆ Understand the given and implied messages of the film clip	◆ Attention – filling in the key words in the correct column while watching the film clip ◆ Language – processing the language in the film clip; filling in the key words used in the film clip; using words to relay images noticed in the film clip ◆ Memory – remembering text and images in the video clip while filling in the worksheet; remembering the lesson demands ◆ Cognition – understanding the ACE newscast message; finding the right words to relay impressions from the images ◆ Sequencing – following the directions on the worksheet; watching the clip while filling in the correct worksheet columns	◆ Culture and Cultural Diversity (NCSS) ◆ Time, Continuity, and Change (NCSS) ◆ People, Places, and Environments (NCSS) ◆ Individual Development and Identity (NCSS) ◆ Individuals, Groups, and Institutions (NCSS) ◆ Power, Authority, and Governance (NCSS) ◆ Production, Distribution, and Consumption (NCSS) ◆ Global Connections (NCSS) ◆ Civic Ideals and Practices (NCSS) ◆ Integration of Knowledge and Ideas (R/LA) ◆ Key Ideas and Details (R/LA) ◆ Compare and Contrast Content (R/LA)
In groups, students fill in the last column ("For discussion"), then meet back with the class and present/ follow the three groups' presentations.	◆ Remember what "news item" your group was responsible for ◆ Recall specific details from the book and film to answer the worksheet questions ◆ Understand the book characters well enough to relay how they would have reacted to the film clip ◆ Relay your group's responses ◆ Follow as other groups present their responses	◆ Attention – responding to the appropriate "news item" assigned; noticing details from the clip and book to best support opinions and responses; following as own group and other groups present their responses ◆ Language – processing the questions asked and relaying comprehensible responses (both in writing and orally when the group presents their answers to the rest of the class) ◆ Memory – remembering what "news items" your group was responsible for; remembering enough details from the film and book to best answer the questions; remembering what other groups responded ◆ Cognition – understanding the ACE newscast message and *Resistance*; finding the right words to relay impressions from the film and book; following what other groups present ◆ Sequencing – following the directions on the worksheet; following the other groups' presentations	◆ Culture and Cultural Diversity (NCSS) ◆ Time, Continuity, and Change (NCSS) ◆ People, Places, and Environments (NCSS) ◆ Individual Development and Identity (NCSS) ◆ Individuals, Groups, and Institutions (NCSS) ◆ Power, Authority, and Governance (NCSS) ◆ Production, Distribution, and Consumption (NCSS) ◆ Global Connections (NCSS) ◆ Civic Ideals and Practices (NCSS) ◆ Integration of Knowledge and Ideas (R/LA) ◆ Craft and Structure (R/LA) ◆ Key Ideas and Details (R/LA) ◆ Compare and Contrast Content (R/LA)

(continued)

Teacher's Instruction	Task Demands On Students	Skills Involved	Common Core Standards*
Have a concluding discussion on the role of propaganda.	◆ Compare the verbal and visual messages in the ACE newscast with those portrayed in *Resistance* ◆ Evaluate how book and film images affect, influence, and change the verbal message presented ◆ Analyze how effective the ACE newscast message might have been on Jacques or the Tessier family ◆ Discuss and evaluate the role propaganda played during WWII and can play today	◆ Attention – following the flow of the class discussion; recognizing nuances in the film and book's art that influence and/or change the verbal message ◆ Language – decoding the verbal messages in the film and book and matching them to the visual images; communicating your own ideas and impressions; following classmates' impressions and ideas ◆ Memory – recalling the verbal and visual messages of the book and film; recalling what the class is discussing; ◆ Cognition – understanding the verbal and visual messages; comparing and contrasting the messages; evaluating how the messages might differ; and comprehending the role propaganda can play ◆ Sequencing – following the sequence of the class discussion; understanding how time may or may not affect the use and distribution of propaganda materials; and understanding and relating cause and effect details	◆ Culture and Cultural Diversity (NCSS) ◆ Time, Continuity, and Change (NCSS) ◆ People, Places, and Environments (NCSS) ◆ Individual Development and Identity (NCSS) ◆ Individuals, Groups, and Institutions (NCSS) ◆ Power, Authority, and Governance (NCSS) ◆ Production, Distribution, and Consumption (NCSS) ◆ Global Connections (NCSS) ◆ Civic Ideals and Practices (NCSS) ◆ Integration of Knowledge and Ideas (R/LA) ◆ Craft and Structure (R/LA) ◆ Key Ideas and Details (R/LA) ◆ Compare and Contrast Content (R/LA)

*Note: NCSS = National Council for the Social Studies Teaching Standards; R/LA = Reading Standards for Literacy in Social Studies

How graphic novels help our five students in social studies

Memory Megan has weaknesses in memory (long-term memory, active-working memory, and short-term memory). Typically, in social studies, students like Megan exhibit difficulty remembering important names (of historical figures, institutions, and geographic locations) and dates of historical significance. Forgetting names, dates, and essential details makes it difficult to analyze what is read and said about campaigns, differences between bodies of governance, cultural and temporal changes, and global connections.

Graphic novels' pairing of visual and verbal information establishes additional memory associations, making the terms, dates, and names easier to retrieve. Furthermore, the detailed illustrations help make the material more personal and inviting. The more students can personally relate to the subject matter, the more memory associations and channels are created.

Attention Andy has difficulty sustaining his focus and attention and is easily distracted. It is therefore challenging for him to follow stories in history; attend to the details and nuances of campaigns, institutions, or events; or even follow lesson instructions and discussions.

Graphic novels provide a means of relaying pertinent information in short visual and verbal bursts. Also, because the visual content adds important information, students like Andy willingly slow down as they look and process multi-sensory details and information. Furthermore, the panels are entertaining and the visual information more personal, inviting attention and focus as readers integrate and evaluate content.

Cognitive Coby exhibits weaknesses with higher-order cognition (critical thinking, analyzing, problem solving, and brainstorming). Typically, students like Coby have trouble evaluating, comparing, and contrasting information; recognizing patterns in history and behavior; and interpreting inferences. This is critical in social studies, as students must evaluate why decisions were made, what was correctly or incorrectly inferred by those decisions, what the ramifications of those decisions were, and what other options might have been possible.

Graphic novels are helpful for students like Coby because the visual details in the art reinforce the verbal message. They make historical details and motives more obvious, and they are easier to decipher with the multi-sensory data. The vibrant, visual component of graphic novels helps delineate and clarify ideas while making reading about the historical events more fun. Furthermore, in graphic novels, character motives are stated and/or implied in the text and art, and readers must integrate the visual and verbal components. This act of constructing and integrating information makes learning and remembering more personal, more meaningful and, as a result, more powerful. It also provides concrete opportunities to construct information and make inferences.

Language Larry has difficulty interpreting and understanding what he reads and hears (receptive language) and explaining his ideas when he speaks and writes (expressive language). This makes social studies more challenging as lessons rely predominantly on language—reading, evaluating, and discussing text.

Graphic novels are an excellent language and learning tool for students like Larry as the visual component supports, reinforces, and further develops the verbal message. The concise language of the text and dialogue balloons make it easier to get the main idea, and the details in the illustrations help students weak in language grasp social and communication nuances. Furthermore, because there is less language-based text, reading is less overwhelming, and it empowers weak language learners to keep up and participate more. Finally, the vocabulary in graphic novels is often more sophisticated than what weak language learners read independently, and the accompanying illustrations help them recognize, decode, and comprehend the vocabulary. As a result, reading becomes less daunting and more rewarding while addressing Common Core reading standards.

Sequential Sue has difficulty remembering and following sequences of information and data. This makes studying historical events more challenging because in order to fully grasp consequences of historical campaigns and events, students must understand the sequence of behaviors, actions, and decisions leading up to these events. Remembering dates is also essential when studying histories and cultures, which is often challenging for students with weak sequential processing skills.

Graphic novels are excellent learning tools for students with sequential processing weaknesses. Reading graphic novels is all about following and integrating small verbal and visual story chunks. The illustrations and story lines are motivating while the following of panels ensures students practice using and tweaking their developing sequencing skills. Furthermore, there is added value with using graphic novels as the verbal and visual cues complement each other and reinforce the sequence of events. Recognizing, following, and understanding the sequence of events is particularly important for social studies as students must remember sequences in history and understand what led up to the conflicts and resolutions of that particular time and place.

Conclusion and suggested graphic novels for middle-school social studies instruction

Graphic novels brim with social studies content. They all deal with some form of governance and social organization, identity building, community issues, and concepts of power and authority. Furthermore, the availability of quality nonfiction graphic novels is growing exponentially, and books on American and world history, and biographies are easier and easier to find. Once found, these graphic novels can be used to introduce and/or reinforce topics in history while inviting student readers to interact on more personal levels with historical figures and characters. These books are motivating and meet diverse student needs and affinities, and they are easily integrated into social studies curricula.

Following is a list of our favorite graphic novels, along with suggested reading grade levels, and the social studies and reading Common Core Standards these books address. As the number of nonfiction and historical-fiction graphic novels being published is rapidly expanding, please check with your librarian or booksellers for even more current choices.

Figure 5.3: A middle-level cross-index of thematically identified and standards-aligned social studies graphic novels

Title and Author	Grade Level	Social Studies Standards	Reading Standards
American Born Chinese by Gene Luen Yang	4+	✦ Culture and Cultural Diversity ✦ Time, Continuity, and Change ✦ People, Places, and Environments ✦ Individual Development and Identity ✦ Power, Authority, and Governance ✦ Civic Ideals and Practices	✦ Key Ideas and Details ✦ Craft and Structure ✦ Integration of Knowledge and Ideas ✦ Fluency Presentation of Knowledge and Ideas ✦ Range of Reading and Level of Text Complexity
Americus by MK Reed and Jonathan Hill	5+	✦ Culture and Cultural Diversity ✦ People, Places, and Environments ✦ Individual Development and Identity ✦ Individuals, Groups, and Institutions ✦ Power, Authority, and Governance ✦ Civic Ideals and Practices ✦ Time, Continuity, and Change	✦ Key Ideas and Details Craft and Structure ✦ Integration of Knowledge and Ideas ✦ Fluency ✦ Presentation of Knowledge and Ideas ✦ Range of Reading and Level of Text Complexity
Astronaut Academy: Zero Gravity by Dave Roman	4–6	✦ Culture and Cultural Diversity ✦ Time, Continuity, and Change ✦ People, Places, and Environments ✦ Individual Development and Identity ✦ Individuals, Groups, and Institutions ✦ Power, Authority, and Governance ✦ Global Connections	✦ Key Ideas and Details ✦ Craft and Structure ✦ Integration of Knowledge and Ideas ✦ Fluency ✦ Presentation of Knowledge and Ideas ✦ Range of Reading and Level of Text Complexity
Bake Sale by Sara Varon	4+	✦ Culture and Cultural Diversity ✦ People, Places, and Environments ✦ Individual Development and Identity ✦ Individuals, Groups, and Institutions ✦ Civic Ideals and Practices	✦ Key Ideas and Details ✦ Craft and Structure ✦ Integration of Knowledge and Ideas ✦ Fluency ✦ Presentation of Knowledge and Ideas ✦ Range of Reading and Level of Text Complexity

(continued)

Using Content-Area Graphic Texts for Learning

Title and Author	Grade Level	Social Studies Standards	Reading Standards
BB Wolf and the Three LPs by J.D. Arnold and Rich Koslowski	8+	✦ Culture and Cultural Diversity ✦ Time, Continuity, and Change ✦ People, Places, and Environments ✦ Individual Development and Identity ✦ Individuals, Groups, and Institutions ✦ Power, Authority, and Governance ✦ Civic Ideals and Practices	✦ Key Ideas and Details ✦ Craft and Structure ✦ Integration of Knowledge and Ideas ✦ Fluency ✦ Presentation of Knowledge and Ideas ✦ Range of Reading and Level of Text Complexity
City of Spies by Susan Kim and Laurence Klavan	5–8	✦ Culture and Cultural Diversity ✦ Time, Continuity, and Change ✦ People, Places, and Environments ✦ Individual Development and Identity ✦ Individuals, Groups, and Institutions ✦ Power, Authority, and Governance ✦ Civic Ideals and Practices	✦ Key Ideas and Details ✦ Craft and Structure ✦ Integration of Knowledge and Ideas ✦ Fluency ✦ Presentation of Knowledge and Ideas ✦ Range of Reading and Level of Text Complexity
Crogan's March (Crogan Adventures, Vol. 2)* Crogan's Vengeance (Crogan Adventures, Vol. 1)* by Chris Schweizer	6–8	✦ Culture and Cultural Diversity ✦ Time, Continuity, and Change ✦ People, Places, and Environments ✦ Individual Development and Identity ✦ Individuals, Groups, and Institutions ✦ Power, Authority, and Governance ✦ Civic Ideals and Practices	✦ Key Ideas and Details ✦ Craft and Structure ✦ Integration of Knowledge and Ideas ✦ Fluency ✦ Presentation of Knowledge and Ideas ✦ Range of Reading and Level of Text Complexity
Journey into Mohawk Country by George O'Connor	4–8	✦ Culture and Cultural Diversity ✦ Time, Continuity, and Change ✦ People, Places, and Environments ✦ Individual Development and Identity ✦ Individuals, Groups, and Institutions ✦ Power, Authority, and Governance ✦ Productions, Distribution, and Consumption ✦ Global Connections ✦ Civic Ideals and Practices	✦ Key Ideas and Details ✦ Craft and Structure ✦ Integration of Knowledge and Ideas ✦ Fluency ✦ Presentation of Knowledge and Ideas ✦ Range of Reading and Level of Text Complexity

(continued)

Title and Author	Grade Level	Social Studies Standards	Reading Standards
Laika by Nick Abadzis	6–8	✦ Culture and Cultural Diversity ✦ Time, Continuity, and Change ✦ People, Places, and Environments ✦ Individual Development and Identity ✦ Individuals, Groups, and Institutions ✦ Power, Authority, and Governance ✦ Productions, Distribution, and Consumption ✦ Global Connections ✦ Civic Ideals and Practices	✦ Key Ideas aand Details ✦ Craft and Structure ✦ Integration of Knowledge and Ideas ✦ Fluency ✦ Presentation of Knowledge and Ideas ✦ Range of Reading and Level of Text Complexity
Lewis and Clark by Nick Bertozzi	5–8	✦ Culture and Cultural Diversity ✦ Time, Continuity, and Change ✦ People, Places, and Environments ✦ Individual Development and Identity ✦ Individuals, Groups, and Institutions ✦ Power, Authority, and Governance ✦ Productions, Distribution, and Consumption ✦ Global Connections ✦ Civic Ideals and Practices	✦ Key Ideas and Details ✦ Craft and Structure ✦ Integration of Knowledge and Ideas ✦ Fluency ✦ Presentation of Knowledge and Ideas ✦ Range of Reading and Level of Text Complexity
Malcolm X: A Graphic Biography by Andrew Helfer and Randy DuBurke	6+	✦ Culture and Cultural Diversity ✦ Time, Continuity, and Change ✦ People, Places, and Environments ✦ Individual Development and Identity ✦ Individuals, Groups, and Institutions ✦ Power, Authority, and Governance ✦ Productions, Distribution, and Consumption ✦ Global Connections ✦ Civic Ideals and Practices	✦ Key Ideas and Details ✦ Craft and Structure ✦ Integration of Knowledge and Ideas ✦ Fluency ✦ Presentation of Knowledge and Ideas ✦ Range of Reading and Level of Text Complexity
Marathon by Boaz Yakin and Joe Infurnari	6+	✦ Culture and Cultural Diversity ✦ Time, Continuity, and Change ✦ People, Places, and Environments ✦ Individual Development and Identity ✦ Individuals, Groups, and Institutions ✦ Power, Authority, and Governance ✦ Civic Ideals and Practices	✦ Key Ideas and Details ✦ Craft and Structure ✦ Integration of Knowledge and Ideas ✦ Fluency ✦ Presentation of Knowledge and Ideas ✦ Range of Reading and Level of Text Complexity

(continued)

Using Content-Area Graphic Texts for Learning

Title and Author	Grade Level	Social Studies Standards	Reading Standards
Mouse Guard by David Petersen	4–8	✦ Culture and Cultural Diversity ✦ Time, Continuity, and Change ✦ People, Places, and Environments ✦ Individual Development and Identity ✦ Individuals, Groups, and Institutions ✦ Power, Authority, and Governance ✦ Productions, Distribution, and Consumption ✦ Global Connections ✦ Civic Ideals and Practices	✦ Key Ideas and Details ✦ Craft and Structure ✦ Integration of Knowledge and Ideas ✦ Fluency ✦ Presentation of Knowledge and Ideas ✦ Range of Reading and Level of Text Complexity
Mush! Sled Dogs with Issues by Glenn Eichler and Joe Infurnari	7+	✦ Culture and Cultural Diversity ✦ Time, Continuity, and Change ✦ People, Places, and Environments ✦ Individual Development and Identity ✦ Individuals, Groups, and Institutions ✦ Power, Authority, and Governance ✦ Productions, Distribution, and Consumption	✦ Key Ideas and Details ✦ Craft and Structure ✦ Integration of Knowledge and Ideas ✦ Fluency ✦ Presentation of Knowledge and Ideas ✦ Range of Reading and Level of Text Complexity
Northwest Passage by Scott Chantler	5–8	✦ Culture and Cultural Diversity ✦ Time, Continuity, and Change ✦ People, Places, and Environments ✦ Individual Development and Identity ✦ Individuals, Groups, and Institutions ✦ Power, Authority, and Governance ✦ Productions, Distribution, and Consumption ✦ Global Connections ✦ Civic Ideals and Practices	✦ Key Ideas and Details ✦ Craft and Structure ✦ Integration of Knowledge and Ideas ✦ Fluency ✦ Presentation of Knowledge and Ideas ✦ Range of Reading and Level of Text Complexity
Page by Paige by Laura Gulledge	5+	✦ Culture and Cultural Diversity ✦ Time, Continuity, and Change ✦ People, Places, and Environments ✦ Individual Development and Identity ✦ Individuals, Groups, and Institutions ✦ Power, Authority, and Governance ✦ Productions, Distribution, and Consumption ✦ Civic Ideals and Practices	✦ Key Ideas and Details ✦ Craft and Structure ✦ Integration of Knowledge and Ideas ✦ Fluency ✦ Presentation of Knowledge and Ideas ✦ Range of Reading and Level of Text Complexity

(continued)

Title and Author	Grade Level	Social Studies Standards	Reading Standards
Play Ball, written by Nunzio DeFilippis and Christina Weir; illustrated by Jackie Lewis	5+	✦ Culture and Cultural Diversity ✦ Time, Continuity, and Change ✦ People, Places, and Environments ✦ Individual Development and Identity ✦ Individuals, Groups, and Institutions ✦ Power, Authority, and Governance ✦ Productions, Distribution, and Consumption ✦ Civic Ideals and Practices	✦ Key Ideas and Details ✦ Craft and Structure ✦ Integration of Knowledge and Ideas ✦ Fluency ✦ Presentation of Knowledge and Ideas ✦ Range of Reading and Level of Text Complexity
Resistance: Book 1* by Carla Jablonski and Leland Purvis	4–8	✦ Culture and Cultural Diversity ✦ Time, Continuity, and Change ✦ People, Places, and Environments ✦ Individual Development and Identity ✦ Individuals, Groups, and Institutions ✦ Power, Authority, and Governance ✦ Productions, Distribution, and Consumption ✦ Global Connections ✦ Civic Ideals and Practices	✦ Key Ideas and Details ✦ Craft and Structure ✦ Integration of Knowledge and Ideas ✦ Fluency ✦ Presentation of Knowledge and Ideas ✦ Range of Reading and Level of Text Complexity
Rust: Visitor in the Field by Royden Lepp	4–8	✦ Culture and Cultural Diversity ✦ Time, Continuity, and Change ✦ People, Places, and Environments ✦ Individual Development and Identity ✦ Individuals, Groups, and Institutions ✦ Power, Authority, and Governance ✦ Productions, Distribution, and Consumption ✦ Global Connections ✦ Civic Ideals and Practices	✦ Key Ideas and Details ✦ Craft and Structure ✦ Integration of Knowledge and Ideas ✦ Fluency ✦ Presentation of Knowledge and Ideas ✦ Range of Reading and Level of Text Complexity

(continued)

Using Content-Area Graphic Texts for Learning

Title and Author	Grade Level	Social Studies Standards	Reading Standards
The Silence of Our Friends: The Civil Rights Struggle Was Never Black and White by Mark Long, Jim Demonakos, and Nate Powell	6+	✦ Culture and Cultural Diversity ✦ Time, Continuity, and Change ✦ People, Places, and Environments ✦ Individual Development and Identity ✦ Individuals, Groups, and Institutions ✦ Power, Authority, and Governance ✦ Productions, Distribution, and Consumption ✦ Global Connections ✦ Civic Ideals and Practices	✦ Key Ideas and Details ✦ Craft and Structure ✦ Integration of Knowledge and Ideas ✦ Fluency ✦ Presentation of Knowledge and Ideas ✦ Range of Reading and Level of Text Complexity
The Sons of Liberty #1 by Alexander Lagos and Joseph Lagos*	6–8	✦ Culture and Cultural Diversity ✦ Time, Continuity, and Change ✦ People, Places, and Environments ✦ Individual Development and Identity ✦ Individuals, Groups, and Institutions ✦ Power, Authority, and Governance ✦ Productions, Distribution, and Consumption ✦ Global Connections ✦ Civic Ideals and Practices	✦ Key Ideas and Details ✦ Craft and Structure ✦ Integration of Knowledge and Ideas ✦ Fluency ✦ Presentation of Knowledge and Ideas ✦ Range of Reading and Level of Text Complexity
Treasure Island, adapted by Andrew Harrar and Richard Kohlrus	6–8	✦ Culture and Cultural Diversity ✦ Time, Continuity, and Change ✦ People, Places, and Environments ✦ Individual Development and Identity ✦ Individuals, Groups, and Institutions ✦ Power, Authority, and Governance ✦ Productions, Distribution, and Consumption ✦ Global Connections ✦ Civic Ideals and Practices	✦ Key Ideas and Details ✦ Craft and Structure ✦ Integration of Knowledge and Ideas ✦ Fluency ✦ Presentation of Knowledge and Ideas ✦ Range of Reading and Level of Text Complexity

(continued)

Title and Author	Grade Level	Social Studies Standards	Reading Standards
Tribes: The Dog Years by Michael Geszel and Peter Spinetta; art by Inaki Miranda	8+	✦ Culture and Cultural Diversity ✦ Time, Continuity, and Change ✦ People, Places, and Environments ✦ Individual Development and Identity ✦ Individuals, Groups, and Institutions ✦ Power, Authority, and Governance ✦ Productions, Distribution, and Consumption ✦ Global Connections ✦ Civic Ideals and Practices	✦ Key Ideas and Details ✦ Craft and Structure ✦ Integration of Knowledge and Ideas ✦ Fluency ✦ Presentation of Knowledge and Ideas ✦ Range of Reading and Level of Text Complexity
The United States Constitution: A Graphic Adaptation by Jonathan Hennessey and Aaron McConnell	5+	✦ Culture and Cultural Diversity ✦ Time, Continuity, and Change ✦ People, Places, and Environments ✦ Individual Development and Identity ✦ Individuals, Groups, and Institutions ✦ Power, Authority, and Governance ✦ Productions, Distribution, and Consumption ✦ Global Connections ✦ Civic Ideals and Practices	✦ Key Ideas and Details ✦ Craft and Structure ✦ Integration of Knowledge and Ideas ✦ Fluency ✦ Presentation of Knowledge and Ideas ✦ Range of Reading and Level of Text Complexity
Zeus: King of the Gods* by George O'Connor	6–8	✦ Culture and Cultural Diversity ✦ Time, Continuity, and Change ✦ People, Places, and Environments ✦ Individual Development and Identity ✦ Individuals, Groups, and Institutions ✦ Power, Authority, and Governance ✦ Global Connections ✦ Civic Ideals and Practices	✦ Key Ideas and Details ✦ Craft and Structure ✦ Integration of Knowledge and Ideas ✦ Fluency ✦ Presentation of Knowledge and Ideas ✦ Range of Reading and Level of Text Complexity

* This graphic novel is part of a series.

Graphic Novels in the Science Classroom

So many graphic novels integrate science or explore the effect of science and technology in society (past, present, future, and/or parallel) that incorporating them into the science classroom is a logical extension. *Feynman* (2011) relates the Nobel laureate's life as well as his work on quantum physics, the Manhattan Project, and the congressional space shuttle disaster panel; *Laika* (2007) recounts the 1950s space race as Soviets sent the first sentient being into space; *Tribes* (2010) explores the effects of a pharmaceutical research disaster; the *Squish* series (2011) is about what life might be like for adolescent single-celled organisms; and *Zita: Space Girl* (2011) and *The Saga of Rex* (2010) are stories based on hyper drive, worm holes, and life in parallel universes. These are just a few of the many graphic novels that relate science, scientific research and inquiry, earth and physical sciences, and science and technology on personal levels children can relate to and soar with.

Aside from their story content, graphic novels engage readers as they construct and integrate the verbal and visual components of story. This makes content of often-complicated processes and systems easier to grasp and recall. But most importantly, graphic novels capture attention and provide outstanding springboards for learning, questioning, and exploring science as they *make* the content come alive!

To help you integrate graphic novels into your science classrooms, this chapter presents:

1. An overview of how graphic novels can help different student learners tackle science material;

2. A specific, graphic novel-based science lesson plan;

3. A discussion of what the graphic novel science lesson is asking students to do—focusing on curriculum standards and five learning skills (attention, memory, language, sequencing, and cognition);

4. An alignment to the appropriate science Common Core Standards;

5. An illuminating discussion on how graphic novels will help five familiar yet different types of learners succeed in your science classrooms; and

6. A lengthy bibliography of suggested graphic novels for science classrooms.

How graphic novels can help students in science: a general overview

Fiction, nonfiction, and science-fiction graphic novels lend themselves to science classrooms and highlight most of the National Science Education Standards. These standards include:

- ✦ Unifying concepts and processes

- ✦ Science as inquiry (understanding scientific concepts)

- ✦ Conducting and understanding scientific inquiry

- ✦ Physical science (properties and change of properties in matter, motions and forces, transfer of energy)

- ✦ Earth and space science (structure of the Earth system, Earth's history, and Earth in the solar system)

- ✦ Science and technology (distinguishing between natural and man-made objects; identifying a problem; and proposing, implementing, and evaluating solutions)

- ✦ Life sciences (characteristics of organisms, structure and function in living systems)

- ✦ Reproduction and heredity

- ✦ Regulation and behavior

- ✦ Populations and ecosystems

- ✦ Diversity and adaptations of organisms

- ✦ Science in personal and social perspectives (personal health; populations, resources, and environments; natural hazards; risks and benefits; science and technology in society)

- ✦ History and nature of science

Graphic novels illustrate and reinforce these curricular themes. They make the subject matter more personal and allow readers (be they visual or verbal learners) to construct working theories of the history and processes of scientific inquiry. These texts provide multi-sensory channels for memory and cognition skills as they explore the pros and cons of science exploration and technology, investigate how science directly and indirectly affects and influences cultures, and relay characteristics and functions of various living organisms on a multi-sensory level.

Furthermore, the art and visual images in these volumes make the material more personal as they invite readers to participate in the story. Integrating the verbal and visual messages while filling in the gutters' gaps and constructing the story makes reading these books a very active, personal experience. The visual components also complement and reinforce the verbal message, and students find the format inviting and motivating. Finally, just as scientific inquiry demands attention to minutia and observable details, so does the reading of graphic novels. Readers must attend not only to the verbal message, but they have to consciously explore the visual content as well.

Two ways to integrate graphic novels in the science classroom

With these overall benefits in mind, we now take a closer look at how graphic novels can be integrated into science classrooms. There are two ways to easily integrate graphic novels into the classroom: 1) critically read and evaluate truth of content and 2) creatively explore and expand scientific fact and inquiry by constructing a graphic novel.

The first approach is to critically read and evaluate graphic novel content—evaluate fact vs. fiction vs. science fiction presented in graphic novel stories. This type of analysis introduces and reinforces science content as students actively evaluate, compare, and contrast fact and subject matter.

The second approach directs students to construct their own graphic novels integrating specific science themes and facts as they evaluate and explore them further. Constructing graphic novels encourages students to create or expand upon scientific themes relating science fact, science fiction, and scientific inquiry to targeted science content.

In this chapter, we will use *Squish #1: Super Amoeba* as we demonstrate both lesson options: 1) critically reading the graphic novel and 2) creating alternate, true-to-life, science story lines. Following the lesson presentations, we delineate the Common Core Standards the lessons address and the learning demands they place on students. Each of these lesson options addresses Common Core science and reading standards that we detail in Figure 6.3. The remainder of the chapter discusses how the lessons address the learning needs of our five students, followed by a suggested graphic novel reading list.

For our science lesson, we take you to Ms. Hubble's fifth-grade classroom. Students are studying bacteria and their role in our lives and ecosystem. Ms. Hubble has asked students to read about bacteria in their textbooks and is hoping to make the lesson more personal and meaningful to her students while sharpening their critical thinking and creativity.

Lesson option 1: Students critically read a science graphic novel

Goal: To gain a greater understanding of single-celled organisms.

Materials

✦ *Squish #1: Super Amoeba* by Jennifer and Matthew Holm (note that this is a series; we are working with the first book of the series)

✦ Figure 6.1: Science fact/science fiction/study further worksheet for *Squish #1: Super Amoeba*

✦ Note: At the end of this chapter, we have also included optional websites that detail basic bacteria facts, as well as those that discuss helpful and harmful bacteria in greater detail. Since Internet resources change all the time, we listed these separate from the lesson and encourage you, as always, to seek out additional resources.

Lesson Activities

✦ Introduce the lesson, and review what you've covered so far about single-celled organisms.
✦ Discussion:
  ◇ What are single-celled organisms?
  ◇ Where do they live?
  ◇ What is their function within their natural ecosystem?

✦ Introduce *Squish*, a graphic novel that takes science fiction to another dimension: inner space and the life of single-celled organisms.

✦ Have students Read *Squish #1: Super Amoeba*.

✦ Introduce the worksheet (Figure 6.1). Please note that, while we present Figure 6.1 as one sheet, you will need to make multiple copies per student as there are 81 pages in *Squish*. Also note that we provide a sample (Figure 6.2) of how to fill in this table.

✦ Complete the worksheet individually, in pairs, or in groups. Note that this can also be given as a homework assignment that is reviewed together as a class or in groups.

✦ Have a final discussion/debriefing. After the worksheet is completed, ask students what they learned about single-celled organisms. Discuss how these organisms (both helpful and harmful bacteria) actually affect their lives. Then close by asking what students would like to learn more about and how they could do this (such as where they could go to find out more information).

Using Content-Area Graphic Texts for Learning

Figure 6.1: Science fact/science fiction/study further worksheet for *Squish #1: Super Amoeba*

Science Fact/Science Fiction/Study Further Worksheet

After reading the graphic novel Squish #1: Super Amoeba, please fill in the following worksheet.

Directions: Analyze each page's verbal and visual message. Decide what is fact, fiction, or something to study further.

◆ IF the image or text represents a fact about single-celled organisms, write it under the "Science Fact" column.

◆ IF the image or text represents something funny or interesting but is a personification of humans OR is pure fiction, write it under the "**Science Fiction**" column.

◆ IF the image or text presents something interesting or is missing something you want to know more about, write in your interest under the "**Something to Take Further**" column.

Page	Science Fact	Science Fiction	Something to Take Further

*See page 133 in the Appendix for a copy-friendly version of this handout.

99

You may want to use Figure 6.2 on the following page to demonstrate exactly how to fill out the worksheet. Or, simply begin filling in Figure 6.1 together with the opening pages of the book, and have students continue working on their own worksheets afterward.

In Figure 6.2, we demonstrate how to fill in the worksheet based on the panels and text from page 28 of *Squish*.

✦ **Panel 1:** Peggy the paramecium is "walking" (by beating her cilia) to school and bumps into Pod and Squish. Pod is wearing a bowtie, and we see his "internal organs"; Squish is wearing a baseball cap and carrying his books; Peggy is smiling and wearing a bow.

✦ **Panel 2:** Pod (an amoeba) is concerned—he can't remember if he washed his pseudopods ("hands for amoebae").

✦ **Panel 3:** Pod is now panicked that he did not wash his "hands," and we see him rolling away on his pseudopods with great anxiety.

✦ **Panel 4:** Squish (another amoeba "standing" with Peggy) is concerned that they'll be late for school.

✦ **Panel 5:** Pod is seen exiting, saying, "…*if I don't wash my pseudopods, I might get sick and then I'll never solve global warming.*" Squish is annoyed, and Peggy is still smiling.

Using Content-Area Graphic Texts for Learning

Figure 6.2: Demonstration of Squish: Amoeba Power worksheet

Page	Science Fact	Science Fiction	Something to Take Further
28	Paramecium move by synchronizing their cilia to move in a particular direction, beating them at an angle to move forward, and beating them in unison to move backwards.	Amoebas and paramecia do not go to school.	What organelles are inside paramecium and amoebas, and what is their function?
	Amoeba move using pseudopods (meaning "false feet"). They do this by extending pseudopods (using cytoplasmic streaming) in a particular direction and reabsorbing them after they're done moving.	Single-celled organisms do not wear bows, baseball caps, or bowties. They also do not need to wash their hands.	Do single-celled organism need to keep clean? How might they do this?
	Single-celled organisms contain organelles and cytoplasm that are enclosed within their cell membrane.	Single-celled organisms do not carry books.	
	Amoeba often have one or more nuclei (here we see them as green circles).		What do amoeba nuclei really look like?

Lesson option 2: Students create their own science-fiction graphic novels

Note: This may be used as an alternative or auxiliary lesson, taking the book further as students integrate scientific inquiry while creating alternate, true-to-life story lines.

✦ Have students read *Squish #1: Super Amoeba* by Jennifer and Matthew Holm, if they haven't already done so.

✦ Review what students have already learned so far from class and assigned readings.

◇ What are single-celled organisms?

◇ Where do they live?

◇ What is their function? What do they do?

◇ How do they move?

- Discuss what students learned from *Squish #1: Super Amoeba,* and what they liked and didn't like about the graphic novel. Relate that these questions are important because students will be creating their own graphic novels. Understanding what works will make their graphic novels more interesting and effective.
  - What did you like about the book *Squish?* Why?
  - What did you not like? Why?
  - How were the pages and panels organized? Was there always the same number of panels per page? Were the panels always organized in the same manner? How does the panel arrangement affect comprehension?
  - Which were your favorite pages? Why?
  - How did the author/artist separate fact from fiction? Is this important? Why?

- Introduce topics you want your students to research/review and write about (or brainstorm possible topics as a class that students can chose to write about). Here are some suggestions for taking *Squish* further:
  - Relate life as "aliens" invade Squish's world.
  - Enter Squish, Pod, and Peggy (or other single-celled characters) in a college-bowl competition on a variety of pond or single-cell-related topics.
  - Write about an epidemic sweeping the "school."
  - Write about global warming and its effect on the characters' lives.
  - Invasion of the OIL SLICK!

- We recommend that you break your students into groups, instructing them to work together to develop their story and product. While this is not necessary, it will move the project along faster. Different students have different skills and affinities, so they can work together integrating and taking advantage of their various talents.

- Have each group create a working outline. Set a date for students to hand in their outline introducing the characters, plot, and relevant facts they will include in their stories. The outline should also relate the story resolution. Outlines should be handed in to you and approved before moving further.

- Once the outline is approved, students begin working on their books. They may want to work in smaller teams of writers and illustrators and divide the work to complete it within a reasonable period of time.

- Have students share their completed works. They may either present their books to the class or make copies of each book—one for each group. Then, have the groups review each other's work. For each graphic novel review, have students fill in Figure 6.1, noting in each column what is "science fact," "science fiction," and "something to take further."

- Final discussion/debriefing: Review the facts learned, and discuss how and where students might learn more.

The lesson's demands

As indicated in Figure 6.3, our suggested lessons incorporate multiple Common Core Standards and learning skills. Let's begin by examining the Common Core Standards in science addressed in this chapter:

✦ **Unifying concepts and processes in science** – Students learn to distinguish and recognize various single-celled organisms (amoeba, paramecium, planaria) and how to observe and evaluate their form and functions.

✦ **Science as inquiry** – This lesson is all about scientific inquiry as students learn to distinguish fact from fiction, how to pose questions for further study, and how to research and answer many of those questions.

✦ **Physical science** – Students learn to recognize physical aspects of amoeba and paramecium, such as their position and motion of internal and external structures as they move and how they engulf (and digest) food.

✦ **Science and technology** – Students examine and distinguish between natural and man-made objects as they determine fact from fiction; students learn to evaluate facts and evidence as they learn to pose questions for future research and investigation; and they recognize the value of science and technology in our ability to observe and examine these microscopic organisms.

✦ **Life science** – Students examine the characteristics of organisms and the structure and function of their various parts; students evaluate single-cell regulation and behavior within their ecosystems as well as their diversity and adaptations under certain conditions.

✦ **Science in personal and social perspectives** – Through discussion and inquiry, students learn how single-celled organisms impact their own lives and influence various environments.

✦ **History and nature of science** – Students become more familiar with the nature and the history of science, with science technology and microscopes, and with the impact of science as a human endeavor.

Aside from these core science standards, students must also process multiple Common Core language arts standards as they read, write, and communicate their thoughts and findings. We include these standards in the Figure 6.3 on pages 105–107.

Finally, to successfully meet these demands, students must demonstrate their skills in verbal and visual language processing, memory, attention, higher-order cognition, and sequencing of information within each required step of the assignment.

Language skills are necessary to read and follow Ms. Hubble's directions, read required texts, and participate in class discussions and worksheets. Students must also use language skills when evaluating each panel's content in determining if it is fact or fiction and in expressing what they would like to learn more about. If completing the second lesson option, language skills are also necessary in creating, discussing, and writing a story.

Higher-order cognition skills are necessary for analyzing, brainstorming, creating, and evaluating information. In this lesson, they are employed to understand the worksheet and Ms. Hubble's directions, evaluate and discriminate between fact and fiction, and brainstorm what they would like to study further. Higher-order cognition skills are also necessary to follow, analyze, and contribute thoughtful content to the closing discussion. If completing the second lesson option, cognition skills are necessary in creating, designing, discussing, and developing a story as well.

Attention skills are necessary for students to focus on Ms. Hubble's directions and discussions and to accurately fill in the worksheet. In this lesson, students must focus on text and illustration details, and they must maintain focus while brainstorming. Attention is also necessary when filling in the correct portions of the worksheet and while monitoring progress as they work through Ms. Hubble's lesson. If completing the second lesson option, attention skills are also necessary for focusing and following through with an original story.

Memory skills are necessary for students to remember Ms. Hubble's directions and keep their place as they work through the worksheet. Students must also be able to recall and retrieve facts they've read and discussed previously related to single-celled organisms. These details are essential when determining fact from fiction. They also have to recall these details for class discussions. If completing the second lesson option, memory skills are necessary for creating fact and fiction, integrating fact and fiction in a determined plot, and following the new story.

Sequencing skills are necessary for students to follow Ms. Hubble's directions in the correct order. Students also have to complete the worksheet in the correct order as they keep track of recording fact and fiction from the book's panels and pages. Students must follow the flow of Ms. Hubble's introduction and class discussions. If completing the second lesson option, sequencing skills are necessary when discussing and creating a story, art, and panels that flow and makes sense.

Figure 6.3: What is this lesson asking students to do?

Teacher's Instruction	Task Demands On Students	Skills Involved	Common Core Standards*
Review and discuss facts learned about single-celled organisms.	✦ Recall facts heard, read, and seen relating to single-celled organisms ✦ Discuss and relate facts learned	✦ Memory – retrieving facts from long-term memory ✦ Language – expressing facts recalled ✦ Cognition – relating and analyzing facts recalled ✦ Attention – relating new details and monitoring the flow of the discussion ✦ Sequencing – recalling facts in proper order and following the flow of the discussion	✦ Unifying Concepts and Processes in Science (NSES) ✦ Science as Inquiry: understanding scientific concepts and scientific inquiry (NSES) ✦ Physical Science: properties and changes of properties in matter; motions and forces; transfer of energy (NSES) ✦ Science and Technology (NSES) ✦ Life Science: characteristics of organisms; structure and function in living systems; reproduction and heredity; regulation and behavior; populations and ecosystems; diversity and adaptations of organisms (NSES) ✦ Science in Personal and Social Perspectives (NSES) ✦ Integration of Knowledge and Ideas (NSES) ✦ Craft and Structure (R/LA) ✦ Fluency (R/LA) ✦ Key Ideas and Details (R/LA) ✦ Comprehension and Collaboration (R/LA) ✦ Research to Build and Present Knowledge (R/LA) ✦ Presentation of Knowledge and Ideas (R/LA)
Read *Squish*.	✦ Decode visual and verbal data in and between each book panel ✦ Store relevant information on single-celled organisms ✦ Compare and contrast the book's content to what you already know ✦ Focus on the science facts while following the story line, plot, and character development	✦ Memory – rehearsing and storing relevant information while retrieving related facts from long-term memory ✦ Language – decoding verbal and visual cues; comprehending verbal and visual cues ✦ Cognition – relating and analyzing facts read and recalled ✦ Attention – attending to new details while monitoring the flow of the story ✦ Sequencing – recalling facts in proper order and following the flow of the story	✦ Unifying Concepts and Processes in Science (NSES) ✦ Science as Inquiry (NSES) ✦ Physical Science (NSES) ✦ Life Science (NSES) ✦ Science in Personal and Social Perspectives (NSES) ✦ Integration of Knowledge and Ideas (R/LA) ✦ Craft and Structure (R/LA) ✦ Key Ideas and Details (R/LA) ✦ Range of Reading and Level of Text Complexity (R/LA)

(continued)

Teacher's Instruction	Task Demands On Students	Skills Involved	Common Core Standards*
Follow the worksheet instructions and fill it out appropriately.	✦ Attend to and follow Ms. Hubble's directions ✦ Recognize how to fill in the table's rows and columns appropriately ✦ Recall and evaluate facts and fiction ✦ Brainstorm possible directions and content for further study	✦ Memory – remembering directions, facts, and fiction ✦ Language – understanding directions and lesson requirements; relating and relaying facts, fiction, and further study accurately ✦ Cognition – evaluating panel content; comparing and contrasting fact from fiction; brainstorming content for further study ✦ Attention – following verbal and written directions; attending to visual and verbal details in Squish ✦ Sequencing – following sequence of directions; following sequence of panels and pages, all while filling in the correct boxes	✦ Unifying Concepts and Processes in Science (NSES) ✦ Science as Inquiry (NSES) ✦ Physical Science (NSES) ✦ Life Science (NSES) ✦ Science in Personal and Social Perspectives (NSES) ✦ Integration of Knowledge and Ideas (R/LA) ✦ Craft and Structure (R/LA) ✦ Key Ideas and Details (R/LA) ✦ Text Types and Purposes (R/LA) ✦ Research to Build and Present Knowledge (R/LA) ✦ Comprehension and Collaboration (R/LA) ✦ Presentation of Knowledge and Ideas (R/LA)
Follow and participate in the final discussion and debriefing.	✦ Recall what you learned from the book and what was discussed previously about single-celled organisms ✦ Evaluate and discuss how these organisms affect our daily lives ✦ Compare and contrast helpful and harmful single-celled organisms ✦ Review and brainstorm what you want to learn more about	✦ Memory – recalling facts and discussion prompts; recalling what was said in discussions to contribute new/original ideas ✦ Language – following and understanding discussions; relating/expressing thoughts clearly and succinctly ✦ Cognition – comparing and contrasting helpful/harmful organisms; evaluating data; contributing to discussion; brainstorming further study ✦ Attention – following discussions; relating appropriate details at appropriate times; focusing on essential vs. peripheral details ✦ Sequencing – following discussion sequences; understanding and relating cause-and-effect details	✦ Unifying Concepts and Processes in Science (NSES) ✦ Science as Inquiry (NSES) ✦ Physical Science (NSES) ✦ Life Science (NSES) ✦ Science and Technology (NSES) ✦ Science in Personal and Social Perspectives (NSES) ✦ Integration of Knowledge and Ideas (R/LA) ✦ Craft and Structure (R/LA) ✦ Key Ideas and Details (R/LA) ✦ Text Types and Purposes (R/LA) ✦ Research to Build and Present Knowledge (R/LA) ✦ Comprehension and Collaboration (R/LA) ✦ Presentation of Knowledge and Ideas (R/LA)

(continued)

Teacher's Instruction	Task Demands On Students	Skills Involved	Common Core Standards*
Create a working outline introducing: ✦ characters, ✦ plot, ✦ relevant facts, and ✦ story resolution.	✦ Attend to and follow Ms. Hubble's directions, making sure all essential details are presented in the outline ✦ Create viable characters, story line, and story resolution ✦ Research and detail relevant facts	✦ Memory – remembering directions; recalling essential facts; remembering where to find facts not readily available ✦ Language – understanding directions and lesson requirements; relating and relaying facts ✦ Cognition – creating viable characters; developing an entertaining and believable story with a beginning, middle, and end that integrates relevant facts ✦ Attention – following verbal and written directions; attending to visual and verbal cues for viable story and characters ✦ Sequencing – following directions in correct sequence; creating a story that flows logically from beginning to middle to end	✦ Unifying Concepts and Processes in Science (NSES) ✦ Science as Inquiry (NSES) ✦ Physical Science (NSES) ✦ Life Science (NSES) ✦ Science and Technology (NSES) ✦ Science in Personal and Social Perspectives (NSES) ✦ Integration of Knowledge and Ideas (R/LA) ✦ Craft and Structure (R/LA) ✦ Key Ideas and Details (R/LA) ✦ Fluency (R/LA) ✦ Research to Build and Present Knowledge (R/LA) ✦ Comprehension and Collaboration (R/LA) ✦ Presentation of Knowledge and Ideas (R/LA) ✦ Range of Writing (R/LA) ✦ Text Types and Purposes (R/LA)
Design and develop your graphic novels.	✦ Delegate responsibilities for each group member ✦ Determine how to set up pages and panels ✦ Write the story and dialogue ✦ Create art to reinforce and support dialogue ✦ Determine font sizes and shapes for various texts	✦ Memory – keeping story details, deadlines, and facts in mind while working on the project ✦ Language – creating text and dialogue that reflects facts and story line ✦ Cognition – writing, designing, and illustrating viable characters and story with a beginning, a middle, and an end ✦ Attention – attending to visual and verbal details necessary for the viable story and characters ✦ Sequencing – maintaining correct sequence in the story as it flows logically from beginning to middle to end	✦ Unifying Concepts and Processes in Science (NSES) ✦ Science as Inquiry (NSES) ✦ Physical Science (NSES) ✦ Life Science (NSES) ✦ Science and Technology (NSES) ✦ Science in Personal and Social Perspectives (NSES) ✦ Integration of Knowledge and Ideas (R/LA) ✦ Craft and Structure (R/LA) ✦ Key Ideas and Details (R/LA) ✦ Fluency (R/LA) ✦ Research to Build and Present Knowledge (R/LA) ✦ Comprehension and Collaboration (R/LA) ✦ Presentation of Knowledge and Ideas (R/LA) ✦ Range of Writing (R/LA) ✦ Text Types and Purposes (R/LA)

*Note: NSES = National Science Education Standards; R/LA = Reading Standards for Literacy in Science and Technology

How graphic novels help our five students in science

Memory Megan: Megan has weaknesses in memory (long-term memory, active working memory, and short-term memory). Typically, in science, students like Megan exhibit difficulty distinguishing between or remembering processes, names of organisms (i.e., genus and species), recalling important elements, formulas, and dates of historical significance. Forgetting these items makes it difficult to discuss, compare, contrast, examine, and experiment.

Pairing visual and verbal information establishes additional memory associations, making the terms, dates, processes, and names easier to retrieve. Furthermore, the detailed illustrations help make the material more personal and inviting. The more students can personally relate to the subject matter, the more memory associations and channels are created.

Attention Andy: Andy has difficulty sustaining his focus and attention and is easily distracted. As a result, it is difficult to follow processes and procedures, attend to the details and nuances of scientific inquiry and design, or even follow lesson instructions and discussions.

Graphic novels provide a means of relaying pertinent information in short visual and verbal bursts. Also, because the visual content adds important information, students like Andy willingly slow down as they look and process multi-sensory details and information. Furthermore, the panels are entertaining and the visual information more personal, inviting attention and focus as readers integrate and evaluate content.

Cognitive Coby: Coby exhibits weaknesses with higher-order cognition (critical thinking, analyzing, problem solving, and brainstorming). Typically, students like Coby have trouble evaluating, comparing and contrasting information, recognizing patterns in behavior, and interpreting inferences and data. This is critical in science, as students must evaluate what they see, hear, and read as they explore worlds aroundtttt them and relevantly relate experiments and data.

Graphic novels are helpful for students like Coby because the visual details in the art reinforce the verbal message. They make science facts and details more obvious as they are easier to decipher with the multi-sensory data. The vibrant, visual component of graphic novels helps delineate and clarify ideas and processes while making reading and evaluating science more fun. Furthermore, in graphic novels, readers must make inferences as they jump from panel to panel, filling in details of fact, time, and fiction that are not visually provided. This act of constructing and integrating information makes learning and remembering more personal, more meaningful and, as a result, more powerful. It also provides opportunities to construct information and make inferences.

Language Larry: Larry has difficulty interpreting and understanding what he reads and hears (receptive language) and explaining his ideas when he speaks and writes (expressive

Using Content-Area Graphic Texts for Learning

language). This makes science more challenging as lessons and labs rely predominantly on language—reading, evaluating, and discussing text.

Graphic novels are an excellent language and learning tool for students like Larry as the visual component supports, reinforces, and further develops the verbal message. The concise language of the text and dialogue balloons make it easier to get the main idea, and the details in the illustrations help students weak in language grasp content nuances. Furthermore, because there is less language-based text, reading is less overwhelming and empowers weak language learners to keep up and participate more. Finally, the vocabulary in graphic novels is often more sophisticated than what weak language learners read independently, and the accompanying illustrations help them recognize, decode, and comprehend the vocabulary. This is particularly useful with scientific jargon and larger words that are often not English based. As a result, reading becomes less daunting and more rewarding.

Sequential Sue: Sue has difficulty remembering and following sequences of information and data. This makes studying science more challenging as following sequences are essential to any lab work and necessary when following the organic and inorganic processes in life's various ecosystems.

Graphic novels are excellent learning tools for students with sequential processing weaknesses. Reading graphic novels is all about following and integrating small verbal and visual chunks of data. The illustrations and story lines are motivating while the following of panels ensures students practice, use, and reinforce their developing sequencing skills. Furthermore, there is added value with using graphic novels as the verbal and visual cues complement each other and reinforce the sequence of events—whether this is necessary in a lab experiment or simply for following the course of various life forms.

Conclusion and suggested graphic novels for middle-school science instruction

Graphic novels lend themselves to science, science exploration, and scientific inquiry. They explore alternative universes and conventional and unconventional life forms; they incorporate and integrate science and developing technologies; and they comment on the state of our Earth, our environment, and our available resources. Furthermore, the availability of quality nonfiction graphic novels is growing exponentially, and books on science, scientists, creativity, and invention abound. These books are motivating, meet diverse student needs and affinities, and easily integrate, enhance, and reinforce science curricula.

Below is a list of our favorite graphic novels, along with suggested reading grade levels and the science and reading Common Core Standards these books address. As the number of nonfiction and historical-fiction graphic novels being published is rapidly expanding, please check with your librarian or booksellers for the most current titles.

Figure 6.4: A middle-level cross-index of thematically identified and standards-aligned science graphic novels

Title and Author	Grade Level	Science Standards	Reading Standards
Astronaut Academy: Zero Gravity By Dave Roman	4+	◆ Unifying Concepts and Processes in Science ◆ Science as Inquiry ◆ Physical Science ◆ Science and Technology ◆ Life Science ◆ Science in Personal and Social Perspectives	◆ Key Ideas and Details ◆ Craft and Structure ◆ Integration of Knowledge and Ideas ◆ Fluency ◆ Presentation of Knowledge and Ideas ◆ Range of Reading and Level of Text Complexity
Bake Sale by Sara Varon	4+	◆ Unifying Concepts and Processes in Science ◆ Physical Science ◆ Science and Technology ◆ Life Science ◆ Science in Personal and Social Perspectives	◆ Key Ideas and Details ◆ Craft and Structure ◆ Integration of Knowledge and Ideas ◆ Fluency ◆ Presentation of Knowledge and Ideas ◆ Range of Reading and Level of Text Complexity
*Courtney Crumrin and the Night Things** By Ted Naifeh	4+	◆ Unifying Concepts and Processes in Science ◆ Science as Inquiry ◆ Physical Science ◆ Science and Technology ◆ Life Science ◆ Science in Personal and Social Perspectives	◆ Key Ideas and Details ◆ Craft and Structure ◆ Integration of Knowledge and Ideas ◆ Fluency ◆ Presentation of Knowledge and Ideas ◆ Range of Reading and Level of Text Complexity
Feynman By Jim Ottaviani and Leland Myrick	6+	◆ Unifying Concepts and Processes in Science ◆ Science as Inquiry ◆ Physical Science ◆ Science and Technology ◆ Life Science ◆ Science in Personal and Social Perspectives	◆ Key Ideas and Details ◆ Craft and Structure ◆ Integration of Knowledge and Ideas ◆ Fluency ◆ Presentation of Knowledge and Ideas ◆ Range of Reading and Level of Text Complexity

(continued)

Using Content-Area Graphic Texts for Learning

Title and Author	Grade Level	Science Standards	Reading Standards
Laika by Nick Abadzis	5–8	✦ Unifying Concepts and Processes in Science ✦ Science as Inquiry ✦ Physical Science ✦ Science and Technology ✦ Life Science ✦ Science in Personal and Social Perspectives	✦ Key Ideas and Details ✦ Craft and Structure ✦ Integration of Knowledge and Ideas ✦ Fluency ✦ Presentation of Knowledge and Ideas ✦ Range of Reading and Level of Text Complexity
*Lunch Lady and the Cyborg Substitute** by Jarrett J. Krosoczka	4+	✦ Unifying Concepts and Processes in Science ✦ Science as Inquiry ✦ Physical Science ✦ Science and Technology ✦ Life Science ✦ Science in Personal and Social Perspectives	✦ Key Ideas and Details ✦ Craft and Structure ✦ Integration of Knowledge and Ideas ✦ Fluency ✦ Presentation of Knowledge and Ideas ✦ Range of Reading and Level of Text Complexity
The Saga of Rex by Michel Gagné	6+	✦ Unifying Concepts and Processes in Science ✦ Science as Inquiry ✦ Physical Science ✦ Science and Technology ✦ Life Science ✦ Science in Personal and Social Perspectives	✦ Key Ideas and Details ✦ Craft and Structure ✦ Integration of Knowledge and Ideas ✦ Fluency ✦ Presentation of Knowledge and Ideas ✦ Range of Reading and Level of Text Complexity
*Squish #1: Super Amoeba** by Jennifer L. Holm and Matthew Holm	4+	✦ Unifying Concepts and Processes in Science ✦ Science as Inquiry ✦ Physical Science ✦ Science and Technology ✦ Life Science ✦ Science in Personal and Social Perspectives	✦ Key Ideas and Details ✦ Craft and Structure ✦ Integration of Knowledge and Ideas ✦ Fluency ✦ Presentation of Knowledge and Ideas ✦ Range of Reading and Level of Text Complexity

(continued)

Title and Author	Grade Level	Science Standards	Reading Standards
Tribes: The Dog Years* by Michael Geszel, Peter Spinetta, Inaki Miranda and Eva de la Cruz	8+	✦ Unifying Concepts and Processes in Science ✦ Science as Inquiry ✦ Physical Science ✦ Science and Technology ✦ Life Science ✦ Science in Personal and Social Perspectives	✦ Key Ideas and Details ✦ Craft and Structure ✦ Integration of Knowledge and Ideas ✦ Fluency ✦ Presentation of Knowledge and Ideas ✦ Range of Reading and Level of Text Complexity
XOC: The Journey of a Great White By Matt Dembicki	5+	✦ Unifying Concepts and Processes in Science ✦ Science as Inquiry ✦ Physical Science ✦ Science and Technology ✦ Life Science ✦ Science in Personal and Social Perspectives	✦ Key Ideas and Details ✦ Craft and Structure ✦ Integration of Knowledge and Ideas ✦ Fluency ✦ Presentation of Knowledge and Ideas ✦ Range of Reading and Level of Text Complexity
Zita the Spacegirl* by Ben Hatke	6–8	✦ Unifying Concepts and Processes in Science ✦ Science as Inquiry ✦ Physical Science ✦ Science and Technology ✦ Life Science ✦ Science in Personal and Social Perspectives	✦ Key Ideas and Details ✦ Craft and Structure ✦ Integration of Knowledge and Ideas ✦ Fluency ✦ Presentation of Knowledge and Ideas ✦ Range of Reading and Level of Text Complexity

* This graphic novel is part of a series.

Websites detailing the basic characteristics of bacteria

✦ Virtual Museum of Bacteria: www.bacteriamuseum.org

✦ A report on bacteria written by a thirteen-year-old from Ohio: "Bacteria," www.amnh.org/learn-teach/young-naturalist-awards/past-winners/1998/bacteria

✦ "Bacteria Divide and Multiply": www.cellsalive.com/ecoli.htm

✦ "What Are Protozoa?": www.childrensuniversity.manchester.ac.uk/interactives/science/microorganisms/whatareprotozoa.asp NOTE: This is one of our favorites! It even comes with a quiz and sound effects. Even if you get something wrong, it's fun!

✦ Digital Learning Center: "Microbial Ecology: Home of the Microbe Zoo": www.commtechlab.msu.edu/sites/dlc-me

Appendix

The Appendix includes the following copy-friendly versions of handouts and other reference materials your students will need:

Figure 2.1: An example of a graphic novel panel from
Vera Brosgol's *Anya's Ghost* (First Second Books, 2011) 114

Figure 2.2: Eleven types of graphic novel panels,
definitions, and examples. 114–117

Figure 2.3: The six types of graphic novel gutters 118–120

Figure 2.4: The six types of graphic novel balloons 120–121

Figure 3.2: Space to Earth ratio worksheet 122

Figure 3.4: Instructions for designing a graphic novel page. 123

Figure 4.1: "The Literate Eye" 124–126

Handout: Write an Alternative Graphic Novel Ending (Chapter 4). 127–129

Handout: "I Write It!" (Chapter 4) 130–131

Figure 5.1: World War II French occupation and propaganda worksheet. 132

Figure 6.1: Science fact/science fiction/study further worksheet for
Squish #1: Super Amoeba 133

Figure 2.1: An example of a graphic novel panel from Vera Brosgol's *Anya's Ghost* (First Second Books, 2011)

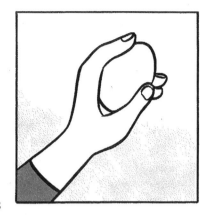

In this panel example, there is a visual, bold-lined boundary, and within that boundary, the reader learns that someone is holding an egg.

With the general idea of the panel understood, teachers and students can move on to the different types of graphic novel panels. There are eleven different types of graphic novel panels (see Figure 2.2.).

Figure 2.2: Eleven types of graphic novel panels, definitions, and examples

Type of Panel*	Definition	Example
Plot panel	Focuses on the action or events in the story	In these panels, readers get a solid idea of the plot. The main character, Anya, is struggling with her coming-of-age identity.
Character panel	Focuses on the people, animals, and/or subjects of the story	In these three panels, the focus is on the characters of Anya and her little brother.

(continued)

© 2013 Meryl Jaffe & Katie Monnin, *Using Content-Area Graphic Texts for Learning*

Type of Panel*	Definition	Example
Setting panel	Focuses on where the story is taking place	In this panel, the focus is on the setting of the kitchen.
Conflict panel	Focuses on the tension in the story	These panels focus on the conflict between Anya's coming-of-age identity crisis and an unexpected source of help.
Rising action panel	Focuses on the events that escalate the tension in the story	These panels focus on the rising sense of insecurity Anya is having about her body image, especially compared to other girls.
Climax panel	Brings the rising action panels to a culminating moment or experience	In this panel, Anya confronts the ghost who really hasn't been a source of help for her identity crisis.

(continued)

Type of Panel*	Definition	Example
Resolution panel	Focuses on the solution to the tension and climax of the story	In these panels, Anya seems to have a more secure sense of self-respect and identity.
Symbols panel	Focuses on images or words that can stand for or represent more than one idea/thing in the story	These panels examine how closely Anya can relate to the ghost, a symbol for herself.
Theme panel	Focuses on the main idea(s) of the story	In these panels, readers get a sense that one of Anya's main concerns is her body image.

(continued)

Type of Panel*	Definition	Example
Foreshadowing panel	Alludes to or insinuates something upcoming in the storyline	In these two panels, the reader learns a key piece of information: the ghost cannot be very far away from her bones.
Combination story panel	Combines two or more of the previously defined panels	In this panel, the focus is on two aspects of the story: the symbolism between Anya and the ghost AND the setting of the well.

*Each panel example is from Vera Brosgol's *Anya's Ghost* (First Second Books, 2011).

Gutters. The gutter is the space in between the panels. In the gutter space, the reader integrates and transforms two ideas (from the adjoining panels) into a single idea; the panels come together to create a continuous, flowing story (Figure 2.3). There are six types of gutters (McCloud, 1993).

Figure 2.3: The six types of graphic novel gutters

Type of Gutter*	Definition	Example
Moment-to-moment gutter	Focuses on moving readers from one moment or instant in the story to the next moment or instant in the story	As Zita informs Joseph that she is pushing the big red button for his own good, the reader sees her from one moment (about to touch the button) to the next moment (touching the button).
Subject-to-subject gutter	Focuses first on one subject and then on another subject	In this gutter example, readers see one character/subject in the first panel and another character/subject in the second panel. From one panel, traveling through the gutter to the next panel, readers see two characters playing "chase."
Action-to-action gutter	An exciting gutter that moves readers from one action-packed moment to the next action-packed moment	This action-to-action gutter shows Zita as she is about to touch the mysterious red button and then, traveling through the gutter to the second panel, as she actually pushes the red button.

(continued)

Type of Gutter*	Definition	Example
Aspect-to-aspect gutter	A gutter similar to tone or mood that pieces together a general feeling about the story	From one panel, through the gutter to the next panel and its gutter, and so on, readers get a sense of Zita's mood, which is nervous and scared.
Scene-to-scene gutter	Links various places and events in the story	In this gutter example, Zita is first shown in a few panels where she is captured by the Scriptorians. Moving through the gutter and into the last panel, the scene changes from Zita's scene to a new scene focused on Joseph as Zita sees that her friend is being held captive and hauled off to some sort of sacrificial ceremony.

(continued)

Type of Gutter*	Definition	Example
Non-sequitur gutter	Typically symbolic and links panels that have a deep, layered thematic meaning in the story; may seem nonsensical, but there is actually some rhyme and reason behind these gutters and their accompanying panels	In these panels and their gutters, readers see the same thing Zita and Joseph see: an unexplainable opening or crack in the air. Unexplainable to them and to the reader at the time, this gap turns into a thematic, transformational, and multi-dimensional opening that drives the plot.

* Each gutter example is taken from Ben Hatke's *Zita the Spacegirl* (First Second Books, 2010).

Balloons. Usually found inside a panel, balloons are the visual spaces where the print-text in the story appears (see Figure 2.4). There are six types of graphic novel balloons (Monnin, 2010, 2011).

Figure 2.4: The six types of graphic novel balloons

Type of Balloon*	Definition	
Staging balloons	Usually informational and set the stage for key elements of the story, such as plot, characterization, conflict, and/or setting	In this staging balloon, the author is describing a character and the year in which the story is going to begin.
Story balloons	Progress the storyline and move it along	In these creative-looking story balloons, the reader learns just how the main character sees the world of science.

(continued)

120   © 2013 Meryl Jaffe & Katie Monnin, *Using Content-Area Graphic Texts for Learning*

Type of Balloon*	Definition	
Thought balloons 	Reveal a character's thoughts (the reader will most likely feel like he or she is reading the character's mind)	In this example, Feynman is pondering the implications of making a new kind of bomb during World War II.
Dialogue balloons 	Words based in conversation and said aloud by the characters	These dialogue balloons show the "fool physicist" speaking to his class.
Sound-effect balloons 	Convey a sense of sound	In this sound-effect balloon, the reader hears the sound of the door slamming shut.
Balloon-less balloons 	Evoke any of the five previously mentioned types of balloons, although not contained by any visual boundary; therefore, balloon-less balloons usually have two labels: balloon-less and one of the other five types	In these balloon-less balloons, which are also sound-effect balloons, the reader hears the characters laughing.

*Each panel example is from Vera Jim Ottaviani's *Feynman* (First Second Books, 2011).

Figure 3.2: Space to Earth ratio worksheet

Space to Earth Ratio in *Laika*

Directions: You will be tabulating all the *Laika* panels in the columns below.

1. **Evaluate** each panel in the book, and decide if it is depicting a scene occurring on or related to land OR one occurring in or related to space.

2. **Enter your data:** When you evaluate each panel as space or Earth, enter a notch (short line), check mark, or "X" under the applicable column below.

3. **Add the entries:** After marking each panel under the "Earth" or "Space" column, add the total notches, check marks, or "Xs" in each column. Write these totals in the "Total" boxes under each column.

4. **Construct your ratio:** Take the total from the space column, and write it on the line above "Space" in the small center box toward the bottom of the sheet. Do the same thing for "Earth." This is your space to earth ratio.

5. **Reflect:** What do you think this ratio tells you? Write your response in the box at the bottom of the page.

Space	Earth
Total:	Total:

	Space	Earth	

What does this number tell you?

Instructions for Designing a Graphic Novel Page

Design a page for a graphic novel with at least five panels. These panels must take up the entire area of the page, making it easier to read and more pleasing to the eye. The five (or more) panels on this page must consist of two or more different shapes. These panels may be circles, rectangles, squares, and/or pentagons.

Formula reminders

A circle's area = pi x radius squared (or πr2)

A square's area = base x height

A rectangle's area = base x height

A triangle's area = 1/2 x base x height

A pentagon's area = the area of a triangle + the area of a rectangle

Page design directions

✦ Write a story in which the number of sentences or story parts equals the number of panels you want to use on your page. This will determine how many panels you will have on the page. (Note that your page must contain at least five panels.)

✦ Determine the area of the page.

✦ Divide the area of the page into the number of panels you intend to make. This number will represent the area of each shaped panel.

✦ Decide which shapes (at least two different types) you want to include on the page and how you want them distributed on the page. Note that different shapes can connote different ideas or impressions. Use these shapes to help emphasize and tell your story.

✦ Draw each of your panels.

✦ Write and illustrate a story to fit in the panels. Use different colors, fonts, and panel shapes to help emphasize points of your story.

Figure 4.1: "The Literate Eye"

THE LITERATE EYE READING STRATEGY FOR MIDDLE SCHOOL ELA STUDENTS

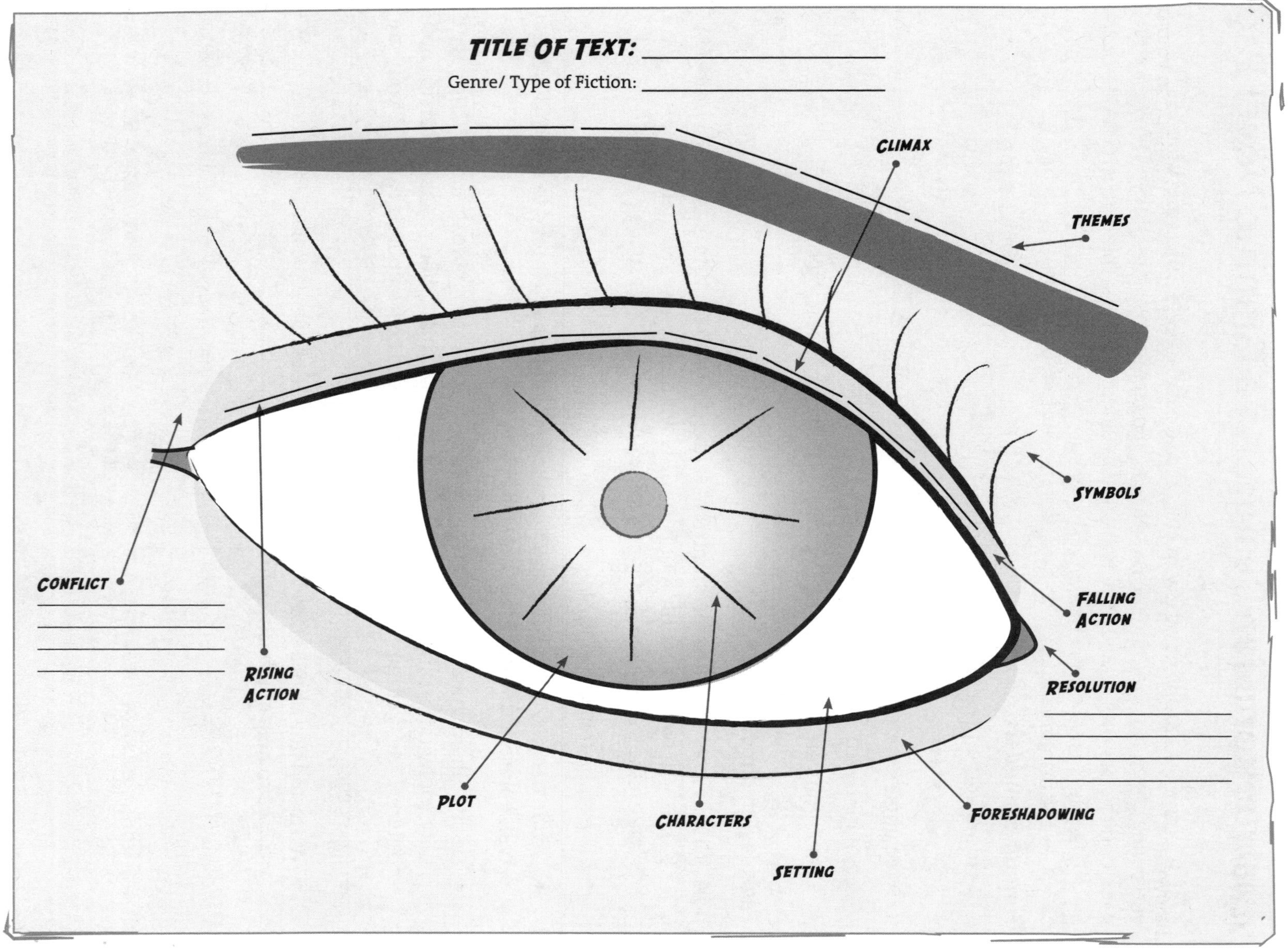

TITLE OF TEXT:

Genre/Type of Fiction:

THEMES

CLIMAX

SYMBOLS

FALLING ACTION

RESOLUTION

FORESHADOWING

SETTING

CHARACTERS

PLOT

RISING ACTION

CONFLICT

THE LITERATE EYE READING STRATEGY FOR MIDDLE SCHOOL ELA STUDENTS

Below each term, in the space on the right, please rewrite this term and its definition in your own words. In the space on the left, please illustrate your definition.

PLOT — the primary sequence of events that setup or tell a story

YOUR ILLUSTRATION	YOUR WORDS

CHARACTER — a person, persona, or identity within a fiction story

YOUR ILLUSTRATION	YOUR WORDS

SETTING — where the events of the story take place

YOUR ILLUSTRATION	YOUR WORDS

CONFLICT — the tension, disagreement, or discord that occurs in a story

YOUR ILLUSTRATION	YOUR WORDS

RISING ACTION — the action or events in the story that stem from the primary conflict and lead to the climax

YOUR ILLUSTRATION	YOUR WORDS

THE LITERATE EYE READING STRATEGY FOR MIDDLE SCHOOL ELA STUDENTS

Below each term, in the space on the right, please rewrite this term and its definition in your own words. In the space on the left, please illustrate your definition.

PLOT — the primary sequence of events that setup or tell a story

YOUR ILLUSTRATION	YOUR WORDS

CHARACTER — a person, persona, or identity within a fiction story

YOUR ILLUSTRATION	YOUR WORDS

SETTING — where the events of the story take place

YOUR ILLUSTRATION	YOUR WORDS

CONFLICT — the tension, disagreement, or discord that occurs in a story

YOUR ILLUSTRATION	YOUR WORDS

RISING ACTION — the action or events in the story that stem from the primary conflict and lead to the climax

YOUR ILLUSTRATION	YOUR WORDS

© 2013 Meryl Jaffe & Katie Monnin, *Using Content-Area Graphic Texts for Learning*

Step 1: Reading Directions

As a class, you will begin by spending three days reading the graphic novel *Americus* by MK Reed and Jonathan Hill. Each day, you will read both in class and at home.

In-class reading

- ◆ Day 1: We will start class on the first day by discussing the key terminology you need to know in order to read a graphic novel (teachers, see Appendix). At the end of day 1, you will be offered independent reading time. Ideally, you will be able to read the first three chapters during the time. If you do not finish reading these first three chapters during class, they become homework reading.

- ◆ Days 2 and 3: On our second and third class days, we will start with 25–30 minutes of independent reading; during this time each day, you will be expected to read three chapters of *Americus*. What you do not finish in class will become homework reading.

- ◆ For the second 25–30 minutes of class on days 2 and 3, you will meet in small groups of 3–4. With your peers, you will be charged with filling out the "Literate Eye" handout.

  At-home reading: Each evening, you will need to finish reading that day's three chapters of assigned reading. Feel free to add to your "Literate Eye" handout while at home as well.

  This daily in-school and out-of-school reading schedule will occur for three days. At the end of these three days, you will have completed your reading of *Americus*, along with your "Literate Eye" handouts.

Step 2: Writing Directions

For the next three days of our language arts class time, you will meet in small groups. In these groups, you will need to reflect upon the written format of *Americus* and, in doing so, become inspired to draft your own alternative ending to the story. The following steps will help you work through the process of writing an alternative ending.

1. How did the writers of *Americus* end their version of the story? Record your group's thoughts in the panel, gutter, and balloon spaces below.

   ✦ The following **panels** (draw or explain) helped me understand the ending of *Americus*:

   ✦ The following **gutters** (draw or explain) helped me understand the ending of *Americus*:

   ✦ The following **balloons** (draw or explain) helped me understand the ending of *Americus*:

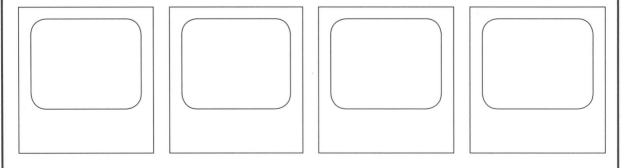

2. Think about the three primary audiences for *Americus*: students, parents/family members and, finally, teachers and/or librarians. What do you think each of these audiences will take away from the ending of Reed and Hill's version of *Americus*?

   ✦ Students –

   ✦ Parents/family members –

   ✦ Teachers and/or librarians –

3. If you could rewrite the ending to *Americus*, which audience would you like to write for?

4. Why would you like to write for that audience? What would you want that audience to think about or know at the end of your version of *Americus*?

5. What elements of story, like those found on your "Literate Eye" handouts, would you need to change or alter in order to convince your audience that your ending is the most valid or logical? Use the "I Write It!" handout from your teacher (teachers, see Appendix, modified from *Teaching Graphic Novels*, Monnin, 2010).

6. **Assessment:** Each group will turn in and present their "I Write It!" alternative graphic novel endings. Each group will also need to turn in their "Literate Eye" handouts.

IF YOU COULD ANALYZE YOUR OWN ENDING, WHAT MIGHT YOU SAY IN RESPONSE TO THE FIVE QUESTIONS OF MEDIA LITERACY ANALYSIS?

1. Who is sending the message and what is the author's purpose?

2. What techniques are used to attract and hold attention?

3. What lifestyles, values, and points of view are represented in this message?

4. How might different people interpret this message differently?

5. What is omitted from this message?

© 2013 Meryl Jaffe & Katie Monnin, *Using Content-Area Graphic Texts for Learning*

GRAPHIC NOVEL PANELS

Figure 5.1: World War II French occupation and propaganda worksheet

News item	List the key words used in the message	Describe the images used with the message	For discussion
"The retreating British army set fire to Lorient's oil tanks … thus harming their former allies … It was only thanks to German firemen … that the blaze was extinguished and the fuel saved."			Discussion: Who would benefit most from saving the fuel? Why? How do you think Jacques (from *Resistance: Book 1*) and the Resistance might interpret this news item?
"In the occupied zone, the Germans are mustering … every able-bodied man to erase all traces of war … Most of the French rail network … is in service again."			Discussion: What were the benefits of the Germans having the French "erase all traces" of the war? How might have the destruction and the rebuilding of Paris affected Sophie, Marie, Paul, and Henri's "mission?" How might it have affected other members of the Resistance in Paris?
"The ladies of the German Red Cross help everywhere … German aid organizations … bring relief to refugees returning to their homes in the occupied zone … food distributions in Montmartre."			Discussion: Describe the faces of the children in this segment of the film clip. Is this food distribution helping them? Why/why not? How is the information in the photo different from the text? In *Resistance*, pages 21–23, Paul's aunt describes the situation in Paris: "They rounded up hundreds—thousands. Mostly women and children. You could hear the crying, the screaming. They kept them there in the Vélodrome d'Hiver for days. No food, no water … My beautiful Paris has changed dreadfully." How does the film's depiction of France compare to Paul's aunt's description?

Science Fact/Science Fiction/Study Further Worksheet

After reading the graphic novel *Squish #1: Super Amoeba*, please fill in the following worksheet.

Directions: Analyze each page's verbal and visual message. Decide what is fact, fiction, or something to study further.

◆ IF the image or text represents a fact about single-celled organisms, write it under the "Science Fact" column.

◆ IF the image or text represents something funny or interesting but is a personification of humans OR is pure fiction, write it under the **"Science Fiction"** column.

◆ IF the image or text presents something interesting or is missing something you want to know more about, write in your interest under the **"Something to Take Further"** column.

Page	Science Fact	Science Fiction	Something to Take Further

References

Abadzis, N. (2007). *Laika*. New York, NY: First Second.

Altschuler, T. (1968). Using popular media to achieve traditional goals. *College Composition and Communication, 19*(5), 340–347.

Amelio, R. J. (1976). American genre film: Teaching popular movies. *English Journal, 65*(3), 47–50.

Appleman, D. (2000). Teaching critical encounters in high school English. New York, NY: TCP.

Bitz, M. (2009). *Manga high*. Cambridge, MA: Harvard Education Press.

Bitz, M. (2010). *When commas meet kryptonite*. New York, NY: Teachers College.

Booth, D. (2006). *Reading doesn't matter anymore*. Portland: Stenhouse.

Brosgol, V. (2011). *Anya's ghost*. New York, NY: First Second.

Buckingham, D. (2003). M*edia education: Literacy, learning and contemporary culture*. Malden, MA: Polity.

Carter, J. B. (2007). *Building literacy connections with graphic novels*. Urbana, IL: NCTE.

Carter, J. B. (2011). *Super-powered word study*. Gainesville, FL: Maupin House.

Clark, R. (1983). Reconsidering research on learning from media. *Review of Educational Research, 53*(4), 445–459.

Eisner, W. (1978). *The contract with God*. New York: Poorhouse Press.

Eisner, W. (1985). *Comics and sequential art*. New York: Poorhouse Press.

Eisner, W. (1996). *Graphic storytelling and visual narrative*. New York: Poorhouse Press.

Fehlman, R. H. (1992). Making meanings visible: Critically reading TV. *The English Journal, 81*(7), 19–24.

Freire, P. (1968). *Pedagogy of the oppressed*. New York: Continuum.

Gardner, H. (1983). Frames of mind: The theory of multiple intelligences. New York: Basic.

Hajdu, D. (2008). *The ten cent plague*. New York, NY: Farrar, Straus, and Giroux.

Hart, A., & Benson, A. (1996). Researching media education in English classrooms in the UK. *Journal of Educational Media, 22*(1), 7–22.

Hatke, B. (2011). *Zita the spacegirl*. New York, NY: First Second.

Hertzberg, Hazel W. (Feb, 1988). *Foundations. The 1892 Committee of Ten*. Social Education, v52 n2. ERIC EJ365372.

Hinton, S.E. (1967). *The outsiders*. New York, NY: Viking Press.

Hobbs, R. (2007). Reading the media: Media literacy in high school English. New York: Teachers College Press.

Howell, W. V., Jr. (1973). Art versus entertainment in the mass media. *Education*, 94(2), 177–81.

Hull, G., & Schultz, K. (2002). *School's out: Bridging out-of-school literacies with classroom practice*. New York: Teachers College Press.

Kinney, J. (2007). *Diary of a wimpy kid*. New York, NY: Abrams.

Kist, W. (2004). *New literacies in action*. New York: Teachers College Press.

Kist, W. (2009). *The socially networked classroom*. Thousand Oaks, CA: Corwin.

Kress, G. (2003). *Literacy in the new media age*. New York: Routledge.

Langer, J. (1998). Thinking and doing literature: An eight year study. *English Journal, 87*(2), 16–23.

Leavis, F. R., & Thompson, D. (1933). *Culture and environment: The training of critical awareness*. Portsmouth, NH: Greenwood.

Maloney, H. B. (1960). Stepsisters of print: The public arts in the high school English class. *The English Journal, 49*(8), 570–579.

Masterman, L. (1985). *Teaching the media*. New York: Routledge.

McCloud, S. (2006). *Making comics: Storytelling secrets of comics, manga and graphic novels*. New York: HarperCollins.

McCloud, S. (2000). *Reinventing comics: How imagination and technology are revolutionizing an art form*. New York: HarperCollins.

McCloud, S. (1993). *Understanding comics: The invisible art*. New York, NY: HarperCollins.

McCloud, S. (2006). *Making comics*. New York, NY: HarperCollins.

Monnin, K. (2011). *Teaching early reader comics and graphic novels*. Gainesville, FL: Maupin House.

Monnin, K. (2010). *Teaching graphic novels*: Gainesville, FL: Maupin House.

Newsom Report. (1963). *Half our future*. London: HMSO.

Ottaviani, J., & Myrick, L. (2011). *Feynman*. New York, NY: First Second.

Pool, I. (1983). *Technologies of freedom*. Cambridge, MA: Harvard University Press.

Reed, MK, & Hill, J. (2011). *Americus*. New York, NY: First Second.

Richards, I. A. (1929). *Principles of literary criticism*. New York: Routledge.

Rosenblatt, L. (1938). *The reader, the text, the poem: The transactional theory of the literary work*. Carbondale, IL: Southern Illinois University Press.

Sachar, L. (2000). *Holes*. New York, NY: Dell Yearling.

Telgemeier, R. (2010). *Smile*. New York, NY: Scholastic.

The New London Group. (1996). A pedagogy of multi-literacies: Designing social futures. *Harvard Educational Review, 66*(1), 60–92.

Wertham, F. (1954). *Seduction of the innocent*. New York, NY: Reinhart.

Index

A

Abadzis, Nick, 26, 27, 90, 111

Adventures in Cartooning: How to Turn Your Doodles Into Comics, 67

Alanguilan, Gerry, 72

Altschuler, Glenn C., 9

Amelia Rules! Superheroes, 67

Amelio, Ralph J., 9

American Born Chinese, 88

American Genre Film: Teaching Popular Movies, 9

Americus, 44, 52–54, 57–60, 63, 67, 88, 127–129

Amir, 72

Amulet, 67

Anya's Ghost, vii, 12, 15, 67, 113–114, 117

Arnold, Andrew, 67

Arnold, J.D., 89

Art Versus Entertainment in the Mass Media, 9

Astronaut Academy: Zero Gravity, 88, 110

Attention Andy, 11, 22, 38, 64, 86, 108

attention skills, 22, 31, 34, 51, 60, 81, 104

Azzarello, Brian, 41, 70

B

Bailey, Neal, 68

balloon
    balloon-less balloon, 19, 121
    dialogue balloon, 19, 65, 87, 109, 121
    sound-effect balloon, 19, 121
    staging balloon, 18, 120
    story balloon, 18, 120
    thought balloon, 19, 121

Bake Sale, 67, 88, 110

Baker, Kyle, 41

BB Wolf and the Three LPs, 89

Beddor, Frank, 69

Beowulf, 67, 69

Bermejo, Lee, 41, 70

Bertozzi, Nick, 90

Big Fat Little Lit, 41

Bitz, Michael, 53

Blackman, Haden, 42, 72

Bone, 67

Booth, David, 5

Boys Only: How to Survive Anything, 67

Brain Camp, 67

Brosgol, Vera, 67

Bruchac, Joseph, 68

Buddha, 67

Building Literacy Connections with Graphic Novels, 5, 53

Buzzboy: Sidekicks Rule!, 67

C

Caldwell, Ben, 42, 72

Cammuso, Frank, 70

Campbell, Aaron, 41, 71

Cardboard, 68

Carter, James Bucky, 5, 6, 53

Cartier, Eric, 69

Castaldi, Elicia, 70

Cat Burglar Black, 68

Cavalier, Liz, 69

Cavallaro, Mike, 68

Chabot, Jacob, 70

Chantler, Scott, 91

City of Spies, 89

Coats, Misty, 71

Cognitive Coby, 11, 22, 38, 64, 86, 108

Colón, Ernie, 40

Comics and Sequential Art, 4

Committee of Ten, 7

Common Core Standards, 21, 25–26, 30–33, 36–37, 40, 43, 73–75, 80, 82, 88, 95, 97, 103, 105, 109

Courtney Crumrin and the Night Things, 110

Creature Tech, 68

Crogan's March (Crogan Adventures, Vol. 2), 89

Crogan's Vengeance (Crogan Adventures, Vol. 1), 89

D

Davis, Will, 68

Dawn Land, 68

De La Cruz, Eva, 72, 112

DeFilippis, Nunzio, 92

Dembicki, Matt, 72, 112

Demonakos, Jim, 93

Deutsch, Barry, 69

DuBurke, Randy, 90

E

Ecob, Simon, 67

Eichler, Glenn, 91

Eisner, Will, 4

Eliopoulos, Chris, 70

Eliot, Charles, 7

English language learner, 54

F

Fajado, Alexis, 69

Female Force, 68

Feynman, 19, 68, 95, 110, 121

Fies, Brian, 72

Fillbach, Matt, 42, 72

Fillbach, Shawn, 42, 72

First Second Books, vii, 12, 15, 18–19, 74–75, 113–114, 117, 120–121

Fiumara, Sebastian, 71

Flight: Volume One, 41, 68

Flood, Joe, 71

Foiled, 68

Forget Sorrow: An Ancestral Tale, 68

Frederick-Frost, Alexis, 67

Freire, Paulo, 8, 9

G

Gagné, Michel, 111

Gallagher, John, 67

Geremia, Daniela, 69

Geszel, Michael, 72, 94, 112

Giarrusso, Chris, 41, 68

Gigantic, 41

Girls Only: How to Survive Anything, 69

Give It Up! And Other Short Stories, 69

G-Man, 41, 68

G-Man: Learning to Fly, 41

Gownley, Jimmy, 67

graphic novel terminology, vii, 1, 11, 19

Graphic Storytelling and Visual Narrative, 4

Guara, Ig, 70

Guay, Rebecca, 70

Gulledge, Laura Lee, 71

gutter

    action-to-action gutter, 16, 118

    aspect-to-aspect gutter, 17, 119

    moment-to-moment gutter, 16, 118

    non-sequitur gutter, 18

    scene-to-scene gutter, 17, 119

    subject-to-subject gutter, 16, 118

H

Harrar, Andrew, 42, 93

Hatke, Ben, 72, 112

Hatter M: The Looking Glass Wars, 69

Helfand, Lewis, 71

Helfer, Andrew, 90

Hennessey, Jonathan, 94

Using Content-Area Graphic Texts for Learning

Hereville: How Mirka Got Her Sword, 69
Hicks, Faith Erin, 67
higher-order cognitive skills, 60
Hill, Jonathan, 44, 53, 57, 67, 88, 127
Hinds, Gareth, 67, 69–70
Hinton, S.E., 44–45, 47
Hobbs, Renee, 8, 10
Holm, Jennifer L., 41, 70, 98, 100, 101, 111
Holm, Matthew., 41, 70, 98, 100, 101, 111
Howell, William J., 9
Huang, Edwin, 71
Huddleston, Mike, 69

I

Identity Crisis, 13–14, 69, 115
image literacies, 5, 8–10
Infurnari, Joe, 90, 91
International Reading Association, 44

J

Jablonski, Carla, 71, 74–75, 92
Jacobson, Sid, 40
Janson, Klaus, 68
Johnson, Dan, 69, 71
Johnson, David, 42, 72
Jones, K.L, 71
Journey into Mohawk Country, 69, 89

K

Kafka, Franz, 69
Kaput and Zösky, 69
Khalil, 72
Kibuishi, Kazu, 41, 67–68
Kid Beowulf, 69
Kim, Susan, 67, 89
King Lear, 69
Klavan, Laurence, 67, 89
*Knights of the Lunch Table: The Dodgeball
        Chronicles*, 70
Kohlrus, Richard, 42, 93
Koko Be Good, 70
Koslowski, Rich, 89
Kress, Gunther, 5, 8, 10

Krosoczka, Jarrett J., 111
Kuper, Peter, 69

L

Lagos, Alexander and Lagos, Joseph, 93
Laika, vii, 26–30, 33, 38, 90, 95, 111, 122
Language Larry, 11, 22, 39, 65, 87, 108
language skills, 26, 30, 34, 49, 60, 80, 104
Leavis, Frank Raymond, 7, 8
Lepp, Royden, 92
Lewis & Clark, 90
Lewis, Jackie, 92
Lex Luthor: Man of Steel, 41, 70
"Literate Eye", 45, 48–51, 56–57, 59, 61–62,
        127, 129
LockJaw and the Pet Avengers, 70
Long, Mark, 93
Lunch Lady and the Cyborg Substitute, 111

M

Making Comics, 4
Malcolm X: A Graphic Biography, 90
Marathon, 90
Masterman, Len, 9
McCloud, Scott, 4
McConnell, Aaron, 94
Meltzer, Brad, 69
Memory Megan, 11, 21, 37, 64, 86, 108
memory skills, 31, 34, 37, 51, 60, 64, 81, 104
*Middle School is Worse Than Meatloaf:
        A Year Told Through Stuff*, 70
Millar, Mark, 42, 72
Miller, Frank, 68
Miranda, Inaki, 72, 94, 112
Monnin, Katie, i, ii, v
Moore, Leah, 41, 71
Mouly, Françoise, 41
Mouse Guard, 91
multiple intelligences, 11
multiple literacies, 5
Murase, Sho, 68
Mush! Sled Dogs with Issues, 91
Myrick, Leland, 68, 110

Index

N

Nagar, Sachin, 71

Nagpal, Saraswati, 71

Nagulakonda, Rajesh, 71

Naifeh, Ted, 110

National Council for the Social Studies,
    74, 85

National Council of Teachers of English,
    7, 44

National Science Education, 96, 107

naturalistic learners

Nicholls, Stan, 71

Niles, Steve, 68

No Fear Shakespeare, 70

Northwest Passage, 91

O

O'Connor, George, 69, 89, 94

Oliver Twist, 71

Oliver, Martin, 67, 69

Orcs: Forged for War, 71

Ottaviani, Jim, 68, 110

P

Page by Paige, 71, 91

panel

    character panel, 13, 114

    climax panel, 14, 56, 115

    combination story panel, 15, 117

    conflict panel, 13, 115

    foreshadowing panel, 15, 117

    plot panel, 12, 54, 114

    resolution panel, 14, 56, 116

    rising action panel, 13, 55, 115

    setting panel, 13, 54, 115

    symbols panel, 14, 116

    theme panel, 15, 55, 116

Pedagogy of the Opressed, 8

Petersen, David, 91

Petrucha, Stefan, 68

Photo Booth, 71

Plastic Man: On the Lam, 41

Play Ball, 92

Plunkett, Kilian, 42, 72

Pool, Ithiel de Sola, 9

Powell, Nate, 93

print-text literacies, 5–9, 44–45

Purvis, Leland, 71, 75, 92

R

Reader Response Theory, 8

Reading Doesn't Matter Anymore, 5

Reed, MK, 44, 53, 57, 67, 88, 127

Remender, Rick, 41

Reppion, John, 41, 71

Resistance: Book 1, 71, 76–79, 82, 92, 132

Richards, I.A. , 8

Robinson, Andrew, 42, 72

Roman, Ben, 68

Roman, Dave, 88, 110

Rosenblatt, Louise, 8

Rust: Visitor in the Field, 92

S

Sala, Richard, 68

Seduction of the Innocent, 3–4

Selznick, Brian, 3–4, 69

Schweizer, Chris, 89

sequential skills, 61, 87

Sequential Sue, 11

*Sherlock Holmes, Vol. 1: The Trial of Sherlock
    Holmes*, 41

Sita: Daughter of the Earth, 71

Skullkickers, 71

Smile, viii, 44–45, 47–49, 71

Smith, Jeff, 67

Space Race, 71, 95

SparkNotes, 70

Spiegelman, Art, 41, 70

Spinetta, Peter, 72, 94, 112

Squish #1: Super Amoeba, ix, 97–99, 101–102,
    111, 113, 133

Star Wars: Clone Wars Adventures, Vol. 1,
    42, 72

Stevenson, Robert Louis, 42

Sturm, James, 67

Superman: Birthright, 72
Superman: Red Son, 42, 72

T

Tayal, Amit, 69
Teaching the Media, 9
Telgemeier, Raina, 44–45, 67, 71
Templesmith, Ben, 69
TenNapel, Doug, 68
Tezuka, Osamu, 67
The 9/11 Report: A Graphic Adaptation, 40
The Baby-Sitters Club: Kristy's Great Idea, 67
The Complete Maus, 70
The Contract with God, 4
The Cryptics, 68
The Dark Knight Returns, 68
The Demon of River Heights (Nancy Drew, Girl Detective #1), 68
The Homeland Directive, 69
The Invention of Hugo Cabret, 69
The Jungle Book, 69
The Last Dragon, 70
The Merchant of Venice, 70
The Mighty Skullboy Army, 70
The New London Group, 8, 10
The Newsom Report, 8
The Odyssey, 70
The Outsiders, viii, 44–45, 47–49
The Picture of Dorian Gray, 71
The Saga of Rex, 95, 111
The Silence of Our Friends: The Civil Rights Struggle Was Never Black and White, 93
The Sons of Liberty #1, 93
The United States Constitution: A Graphic Adaptation, 94
Thomas, Roy, 71

Thompson, Denys, 7, 8
Treasure Island, 42, 93
Tribes, 72, 94–95, 112
Tribes: The Dog Years, 94, 112
Trickster: Native American Tales: A Graphic Collection, 72
Trondheim, Lewis, 7, 8, 69
types of learners, 21, 25, 43, 73, 96

V

Varley, Lynn, 68
Varon, Sara, 67, 88, 110
Venditti, Robert, 69

W

Waid, Mark, 72
Wang, Jen, 70
Weir, Christina, 92
Welsh, CEL, 71
Wertham, Frederic, 3–4
Whatever Happened to the World of Tomorrow?, 72
Wong, Walden, 42, 72

Y

Yakin, Boaz, 90
Yang, Belle, 68
Yang, Gene Luen, 68, 88
Yolen, Jane, 68, 70
Yu, Leinil Francis, 72

Z

Zahra's Paradise, 72
Zeus: King of the Gods, 94
Zita the Spacegirl, 18, 72, 112, 120
Zub, Jim, 71

Notes

Notes

Notes